BEHIND THE CURTAIN,
THE CANDLES BURN

Praise for
Behind the Curtain, the Candles Burn

This book is a jewel of historical memory!

I can assure you that it is unique in its style among books about the Holocaust. The authors skillfully stitch together historical facts and compelling stories.

As I read it, I was absorbed into a wicked world where even the ground cries out for the massive amounts of innocent blood spilled upon it. My spirit was broken beyond tears by the cruelty and evil to which our beloved Jewish people in Belarus were exposed. I was impressed to see how these people who had everything taken from them were reached by the love of Yeshua through the sacrificial service of the Winograds and those who have joined them. I so appreciated the Messianic Jewish perspective with which it was written. This book is part of our historical and cultural legacy!

—Myriam Levy Chernoff, Vice President
of the International Messiah Jewish Alliance

The Winograds are true pioneers who have fearlessly stepped out in faith and embodied the heart and hands of the Messiah toward those who have survived inexpressible loss and pain. Behind the Curtain, the Candles Burn *not only exposes the shocking reality of the Holocaust in Belarus but is also filled with riveting testimonies of how God can turn tragedy into redemption. Read this book from cover to cover—you will be enlightened and also inspired to do even more for your Lord.*

—Wayne Hilsden, Cofounder of Kings of Kings Community,
Jerusalem and President of FIRM: Fellowship of Israel Related Ministries

Wow! I found that I could not put down this riveting book and read it in one sitting. These true stories, filled with important historical details, read like a James Michener historical novel—poignant and brilliant storytelling!

Because we are reading real-life stories of Jewish men and women from Belarus who suffered horrific misery at the hands of the Nazis in World War II, it deeply moved me to know that these survivors eventually found comfort in the arms of the God of Israel and their Messiah, Yeshua.

An amazing book worthy of a full-length movie.

—Joel Chernoff, General Secretary and CEO of the
Messianic Jewish Alliance of America

Stories of Jewish suffering have long gripped my heart. Reading accounts of the shocking hatred and violence my Jewish people have endured is never easy, but such stories hold great importance. They show us the seemingly limitless hate that abounds throughout history and suggest ways in which we should respond. This book tells such stories, gut-wrenching stories of the suffering of the Jewish people during the Holocaust in Belarus and of their perseverance under persecution in the Soviet Union. However, these stories do not leave you without hope. The lives of these survivors were not consumed by the suffering brought by the Nazis and Soviets as they eventually experience the redemptive work of Yeshua, demonstrating that love can overcome even the fiercest hate.

—Dr. Michael L. Brown, author of *Our Hands Are Stained with Blood: The Tragic Story of the Church and the Jewish People*

You can sense the Winograds' deep love and evident respect for the Holocaust survivors they serve in almost every word of this book.

The historical material is well-crafted and provides a great sense of background enabling the reader to better appreciate all these folks endured at the hands of the Nazis and the Communists. The lives of the survivors, so poignantly described, were very sad and difficult to read because of the pain they experienced at the hands of those who despised God's chosen people. Yet, what a joyful conclusion to also read the testimonies of those who found the Jewish Messiah, Yeshua! The healing and joy experienced by those who embraced the Lord were palpable and a testimony to His love and power.

I hope you will not only read this book but share it with others and invite them to pray for the work of the Winograds and their team who faithfully serve the Holocaust survivors each and every day.

—Dr. Mitch Glaser, President of Chosen People Ministries

Behind the Curtain, the Candles Burn

*Recovering the Lost Stories of
the Holocaust Survivors of Belarus*

Stewart Winograd &
Chantal Winograd

with J. L. Corey

LUMINARE PRESS
WWW.LUMINAREPRESS.COM

Printed in the United States of America

Luminare Press
442 Charnelton St.
Eugene, OR 97401
www.luminarepress.com

LCCN: 2021922591
ISBN: 978-1-64388-681-7

To our dear friends, the survivors of the Shoah (Holocaust), to the memory of their loved ones, and the estimated six million Jewish people who perished at the hands of the Nazis and their collaborators.

CONTENTS

Foreword

THE HOLOCAUST IS, WITHOUT QUESTION, THE GREATEST ATROC-ity in modern human history. More than six million Jews, along with millions of other "undesirables" such as the Romani people (commonly known by the derogatory term "Gypsies"), were murdered during a seven-year span from 1938 to 1945. In the case of the Jewish people, they were systematically exterminated for no other reason than they were physical descendants of Abraham, Isaac, and Jacob. Those who survived lived through horrors few can imagine. Many who did make it through this nightmare returned to their towns and villages only to find their homes occupied by neighbors and townspeople who refused to return their property and forced them to move on. They wandered from place to place with nothing more than the tattered clothes on their back. Those who ended up in what became Soviet-controlled Europe continued to be victimized throughout their lives.

When I started to encounter these survivors during my trips to Russia, Ukraine, and Belarus in the early 1990s, I immediately fell in love with them. To my astonishment, instead of being embittered and hostile toward a Jewish follower of Jesus, I found them to be warm, engaging, and gracious. Within hours of meeting them, many invited me into their homes to hear the story of my spiritual journey. Their hospitality and kindness overwhelmed me. They shared the little they had with me and made me feel like family.

When my dear friends Stewart and Chantal Winograd joined me in Minsk, Belarus, for one of our Festivals of Jewish Music and Dance in 1994, they were so moved by what they heard and saw, they quickly moved their entire family to Minsk. Like me, they fell in love with these amazing people, and their lives have never been the same.

As the Winograds served this incredible community in Belarus, they gained the survivors' trust, and many began to share their stories of survival. Hearing one amazing story after another, they realized that these stories that had been hidden behind the Iron Curtain needed to be told.

In a world where a growing number of antisemites try to convince us the Holocaust never happened; I cannot overstate how important the testimonies of these fifteen survivors are. We must never forget, and we must learn from the past, for those who fail to learn from it are doomed to repeat it.

I am deeply grateful to Stewart and Chantal for writing this book and for their dedicated love and service to the survivors. Beyond this, words cannot express how encouraged I am by the fact that almost all of the survivors in this book discovered the love of the God of Israel and new life in Messiah Yeshua.

I trust that reading of the impact of the power of God's love at work in the aftermath of such suffering will strengthen your faith and encourage you as much as it did me.

—Jonathan Bernis
President and CEO, Jewish Voice Ministries International

Preface

THE SHOAH (HOLOCAUST) IS NOT JUST ONE STORY BUT RATHER millions of individual stories of victims and survivors who underwent unimaginable suffering and heroes who faced horrifying evil in the largest mass murder in human history.

Some stories are often told, and some never are. Hidden behind the Iron Curtain, the Holocaust survivors of Belarus (White Russia) have often felt forgotten by the rest of the world. This book tells their story through the eyes of fifteen of our dear friends who number among the survivors.

Their stories span prewar Belarus, World War II, living through the horrors of the Holocaust, living under the Communist regime of the Union of Soviet Socialist Republics (USSR), and life in the aftermath of the collapse of the USSR in 1991. A unique aspect of our book is that it also chronicles the spiritual journeys of these Jewish survivors who had every reason to deny the existence of God but instead, in their old age, discovered that the God of Israel not only exists but cares.

In this book, you will get to know our dear friends as well as their family members, many of whom tragically did not live to tell their stories. You will meet some of the Righteous Among the Nations, brave people who risked their lives and endangered their own families to help Jewish people. You will read stories of courage and compassion. Stories of Jewish children who should have enjoyed carefree childhoods but instead faced death every time they went out to find food for their starving family and friends. You will hear about heroic teenagers who joined the partisans to fight against the Nazis and went back into the ghetto to liberate their people from the ongoing starvation, torture, and carnage.

You will also see that despite the unimaginable suffering, evil, and loss that they experienced, these Holocaust survivors are not bitter. They are warm, caring, and loving people who are full of life. We can all learn from their wisdom, compassion, and strength.

During the twelve years we lived in Belarus, our lives became intertwined with numerous Holocaust survivors, and we developed relationships with them that continue to this day. We visit with them in their homes, celebrate the Biblical Jewish holidays, pay our respects at Jewish memorial sites together, help in practical ways whenever the need arises, and spend time talking about deep topics of life. We have laughed and cried together, and the love we share is mutual. We are more than friends. We are family. We intend to be there for them for as long as we all live on this earth.

The survivors obviously carry deep pain and scars from their experiences. They long for comfort and emotional healing. Through our friendship with them, we were able to play a role in bringing them the comfort and love that God offers through Messiah Yeshua (Jesus).

We believe that God creates every person for a purpose. Looking back on our lives, we perceive that serving and honoring Holocaust survivors and participating in their spiritual journeys was part of His destiny for us. It is a great honor to tell their personal stories and the greater untold story of the Jewish people of Belarus in this book. We believe that like us, you will be moved and inspired by their courage, survival, and the redemptive work of God in their lives.

—Stewart and Chantal Winograd
October 2021

A Few Words
from Our Coauthor

I HAVE ALWAYS BEEN KEENLY INTERESTED IN HISTORY, AND FROM the time I was a teenager, my bookshelves were packed with books about World War II. Thanks to the support of my parents and grandparents, I was able to pursue my passion for history, earning a degree in history from Liberty University and studying abroad in Israel. Visiting Yad Vashem (the National Holocaust Museum and Memorial in Jerusalem) during that time was one of the most life-changing events in my life, one that started me on a quest to understand how such horrors could take place and what could be done to prevent them. In my efforts to understand the Holocaust, I returned to Israel to complete my master's degree at The Hebrew University of Jerusalem in Jewish studies as well as visiting many of the memorials, museums, and concentration camps scattered across Europe. These sites bear silent witness to the horrible crimes and suffering that took place.

However, to understand the Holocaust, one must realize that it is not only a matter of statistics, numbers, or historical details. Of course, all of these are important, but learning about the Holocaust is not only studying historical facts. It is hearing the stories of the people who lived through this dark period of history, reading their names, and gazing at their faces and pictures, recognizing each individual experience. When the Winograds invited me to visit Belarus and meet their friends who survived the Shoah, I got the unforgettable opportunity to experience such stories firsthand.

Belarus is a land steeped in history, and visiting takes you back to another time. Here the most powerful memorials to the Holocaust are not found on street corners but in the cramped yet welcoming Soviet-era apartments where those who survived still live, resilient, yet surrounded by the nightmarish memories of the events of their childhoods. Words cannot express how grateful I am for the opportunity to step into this world. The warm relationships the Winograds have cultivated with the survivors over the years meant a host of open doors and opportunities for me to hear their stories. The Holocaust survivors' family-like fondness for the Winograds is apparent when they speak of the many years of friendship they have shared.

The honor of being able to help bring you these stories is one of the greatest privileges of my life. I hope that this book will do justice to their experiences and suffering, preserving their testimony and the memory of their families and the millions of other voices silenced by the Nazis. May their memories be a blessing and never be forgotten.

—J. L. Corey
Jerusalem, Israel

Acknowledgments

As we lived with the Holocaust survivors and heard their stories, we began to desire to compile the stories of some of our friends' experiences to share with the world. After more than a decade, this dream has come true as the result of some wonderful teamwork.

First and foremost, we want to acknowledge the God of Israel and Messiah Yeshua (Jesus in Hebrew) who granted us the wonderful privilege and opportunity to live in Minsk, Belarus, from 1995–2007 and share life with survivors then and now. He also enabled us to embrace His love and compassion for the Holocaust survivors. It's been an amazing journey.

This book would have never taken its form without J. L. Corey and his gift for telling stories connected to historical events. He joined us in this project to help present the stories in their historical context. As a historian with a passion for the Jewish people and their history, he combined his skill for historical research with meticulous attention to detail. In doing so, he did a wonderful job in making this book not only a collection of biographies of the fifteen survivors we gave him but the accurate historical narrative that you will read. We appreciate his dedication to carefully researching and writing while simultaneously pursuing his master's degree in Jewish history at The Hebrew University of Jerusalem.

We are so grateful for our wonderful team on the ground in Belarus, their hearts of compassion and dedicated service. They have served the Holocaust survivors week after week, year after year: Tanya Gamburg, Anya Vereshag, Dima Selechanov, Vitalik Kondrat, Olga Glushkova, Yulia Klimenkova. Roman Zenkovich, Vladimir Bury, Nina Selchenok, Tamara Mysova, Vadim and Natasha Vyonilo, Valya Svitkina, Svetlana Zubareva, Stephen Singley and many other volunteers who give of themselves and their time to serve бескорыстный (*bes coriznya* means serving and not demanding anything in return).

We want to thank the Reach Initiative International board of directors and everyone who supported us in prayer and cheered us on over the years.

Our appreciation to Olga Kuzheleva, who translated the survivor's written stories from Russian to English, and to Alexey Beroskin for the invaluable knowledge about Jewish history in Belarus that he provided.

Our four children, Joshua, Miriam (who serves Holocaust survivors in Israel), Sarah, and David have assisted us in serving the Holocaust survivors throughout the years. We thank God for each one of them and their compassionate hearts.

A special thanks to our children, Joshua and Sarah, and our friends James Adler, Josh Cohen, and Hylan Slobodkin for using their gift of writing to assist us with proofreading.

We so appreciate Felix Lipsky, Mikhail Canterovich, Mikhail Treister, Yaakov Levin, Mikhail Rosenshien, Valery Myzgayeu, and Yevgeny Andreichuk who have served since 1995 as either chairman or vice-chairman of the National Association of Jewish Former Prisoners of Ghettos and Nazi Concentration Camps. Every one of these people and the members of their leadership team are men and women of integrity and compassion. Their labor of love for all the survivors of the Holocaust is inspirational. It has been a delight to work with each one of them over the past twenty-six years.

We want to acknowledge Frida Reizman, Maya Krapina, Vladimir Trachtenberg, and Joseph Yesalevich. We have been privileged to cooperate with them for the good of many survivors.

Of course, we want to give special acknowledgment to the Holocaust survivors featured in this book: Zoya Oboz, Lova Kravetz, Leonid Rubinstein, Sima Margolina, Lev Gurevich, Anatoly Dikushin, Raisa Naimark, Lydia Petrova, Yelena Bugayeva, Alexander Mysov, Yevsey Shuster, Irina Sussman, Vladimir Sverdlov, Yaakov Levin, and Mikhail Treister. This book would not be possible without them entrusting us with the honor of telling their stories to the world. You are all dear to us.

Most of them transcribed their stories themselves while others recounted their stories to us and our team members. The survivors' ability to recall details of their experience in the Holocaust is more than amazing. The accurate and very personal eyewitness accounts woven together with the history of the Jewish people of Belarus make this book unique. These stories are relevant to Jewish and non-Jewish audiences as well as scholars interested in the Holocaust and Jewish life in post-war as well as post-Soviet Belarus.

We are thankful for the hundreds of other Holocaust survivors who have enriched our lives, the lives of our family members, and so many others!

Survivors Whose Stories
Appear in This Book

———∞∞∞———

YELENA BUGAYEVA was an infant when the war began in 1941. She lived with Varvara and Mikhail Yanushevich in Minsk during much of the war.

ANATOLY DIKUSHIN was twelve when the war began. He survived the Minsk Ghetto and lived in Orphanage Number 7, run by Vera Sparning.

LEV GUREVICH was twenty-three years old when the war began. Originally from a shtetl in Russia near the Belarusian border, he served in the People's Militia and with the partisans in Belarus.

LOVA (LEV) Kravetz was eleven when the war began. He survived the Minsk Ghetto with his younger sister, Maya, and served with the Zorin Parisian Group.

YAAKOV LEVIN was six years old when the war began, living with his parents, Lazar and Vera, and brother, Misha, in Grodno. During the war, he spent time in the Babruysk Ghetto and the village of Palovichi, where he lived with a woman named Irina Masyukevich.

SIMA MARGOLINA was thirteen when the war began. She lived with her parents and younger sisters, Nechama and Berta, in the village of Uzda. She also survived living in the Minsk Ghetto.

ALEXANDER MYSOV was sixteen when the war began, living in Mogilev with his family. He spent the war as a partisan and hiding with the Titova family that sheltered him.

RAISA NAIMARK was eight years old when the war began. She lived in Mogilev with her parents, Samuel and Lubov, before escaping to live in the countryside where her sister, Vera, was born.

ZOYA OBOZ was twelve when the war began and lived in the Minsk Ghetto before serving with the Zorin Partisan Unit.

LYDIA PETROVA was three when the war began and lived in Orphanages Number 2 and 7 in Minsk.

LEONID RUBENSTEIN was thirteen when the war began, living in Minsk with his large family. During the war, he survived the Minsk Ghetto as well as the concentration camps of Auschwitz, Dachau, Majdanek, and Natzweiler-Struthof.

YEVSAY SHUSTER was twenty when the war began and served in the Red Army as a pilot in Murmansk, returning to his hometown of Minsk only after the war.

IRINA SUSSMAN was two when the war began and lived in Orphanage Number 2 in Minsk.

VLADIMIR SVERDLOV was eleven when the war began and was staying in a children's sanitarium in the village of Krynki. Later, he lived with a woman named Aleksandra Zvonnik, who hid him for much of the war.

MIKHAIL TREISTER was fifteen and living in Minsk when the war began. He later served with the partisans.

In addition to the fifteen stories we tell, we mention part of the story of Maya Krapina. Maya was six when the war began and escaped Minsk with her older brother, Joseph, to the village of Porechye, where she lived with a woman named Anastasia Khurs.

Prologue

Our story begins in 1995 in our (Stewart and Chantal) small home in Minsk, Belarus, as several guests gathered around our table lit with the soft glow of candlelight to welcome the Shabbat (Sabbath).

The Jewish people have observed this holy day of rest for millennia, and the scene is a familiar one in Jewish homes around the world. As the sun sets every Friday, candles are lit while prayers and songs in Hebrew fill the air and blend with the aroma of fresh-baked challah (a traditional Jewish bread). The tradition of the Shabbat is an ancient religious practice rooted in the Torah given to Moses and the people of Israel at Mount Sinai.

Although the scene of Jewish people gathering to welcome the Shabbat has been repeated countless times over thousands of years, this Shabbat meal had a special significance for those in attendance. This Shabbat was the first of many celebrations our family would observe in our new home. We and our four children had recently left our home in upstate New York to move to the nation of Belarus. Belarus gained independence four years before as the Soviet Union collapsed. Now the nation sought to rebuild itself after decades of Communist rule and restore the independent Belarusian identity of its people rather than the Soviet one that had been imposed upon them.

For us, a different sort of restoration drew us to this corner of the former Union of Soviet Socialist Republics (USSR). We sought to take part in the spiritual rebuilding of the country and the Jewish people. Motivated by the love of Yeshua (Jesus), the Messiah of Israel, and the reality that He had transformed our lives, we came with a desire to share His love, goodness, and the truths of the Bible to a nation that was broken and in chaos.

1

The collapse of the USSR decimated Belarus's economy, which caused the people to suffer from massive food shortages. We knew that we could not just meet people's spiritual needs but that God was calling us to meet their basic and humanitarian needs as well. The Belarusian people had already lived through some of the world's most horrific evils. In World War II (or the Great Patriotic War, as the Soviets call it), the Nazi Blitzkrieg (lightning war) invasion of the USSR cut right across the fields, forests, and cities of Belarus. Under the brutal Nazi occupation that followed, it is estimated that one out of every four Belarusians died. Every citizen of Belarus experienced the effects of the Nazi invasion, but for the Jewish people, the Nazi's arrival meant they would soon become victims of the greatest crime in human history—the mass murder of the Holocaust. As many as eight hundred thousand Jewish men, women, and children (including as much as 90 percent of the prewar population) perished within the borders of Belarus during the three years of occupation.[1]

Several of these who endured this terrible suffering joined us on this memorable dinner in our home. Felix Lipsky and Mikhail Canterovich served as leaders of the Association of Jewish Former Prisoners of Ghettos and Nazi Concentration Camps. (For simplicity, we refer to it as the National Association of Holocaust Survivors from here on.) The night was particularly significant for Mikhail and for Felix's wife, Sophia, as this was the first time they had been able to participate in the celebration of a Shabbat tradition their people had observed for so long. Around the table, we exchanged stories, sensed a deep bonding with the survivors, and began to realize they would play an important role in our lives.

After our guests left, we wept over the significance of what we had just experienced and the stories we heard. We wept for the Jewish people of Belarus who had been singled out, tortured, dehumanized, and killed by the Nazis because they were Jewish. We wept for those who survived only to suffer again under Communism as their religion, culture, and traditions were outlawed in an effort to stamp out Jewish life in Belarus. The Nazis tried to destroy the Jewish people, and the Soviets tried to destroy the Jewish soul. Thankfully, neither succeeded.

After this first Shabbat dinner, we felt confident that God had called us to play a role in bringing the survivors His healing and restoration. Yeshua spoke to our hearts: "Create opportunities for Me to bring Holocaust survivors comfort. Serve as many survivors that I will enable you to serve for as long as they live on earth. Show them my love."

Map of Belarus

CHAPTER 1

Belarus: A Jewish Home

———— ⌇⌇⌇ ————

To understand the horror the Jewish community of Belarus experienced, one must first understand how this quiet corner of Europe became home to so many Jewish people.

Often persecuted and discriminated against, the Jewish people of Europe were forced to search out safe places to live, raise their families, and practice their faith. For centuries, the Ashkenazi Jewish culture was centered around the Rhine River Valley in Germany and France, where they had settled during the days of the Roman Empire. However, in 1095, Christian Crusaders on their way to the Holy Land ravaged the Rhineland communities. Though long used to living under discrimination, the horror of the violence and hate the Jewish communities experienced motivated many to seek out a more tolerant society in which to dwell. Many migrated to the east. In the Kingdom of Poland, the Jewish people found a place to settle in relative peace.

In 1386, the Polish Queen Jadwiga united her kingdom with the Duchy of Lithuania through the marriage of the two rulers. This union led to the creation of the Polish-Lithuanian Commonwealth, a nation that at its zenith, would be one of the largest in Europe. Thus, the territory of what later became the modern Republic of Belarus came under the rule of the Polish throne, and Jewish people began to settle there. Under this large, multi-ethnic nation, Jewish people lived alongside Poles, Lithuanians, and Belarusians in relative peace with only isolated examples of persecution.

However, after the Commonwealth began to weaken, the neighboring empires of Austria, Russia, and Prussia began to eye the vast lands of the Polish-Lithuanian Commonwealth. In 1772, these three powers made their move and annexed substantial portions of the Commonwealth. This action, known as the First Partition of Poland, was the first step in a process. By 1795, the neighboring powers had carried out two more "partitions" and erased the Poland-Lithuanian Commonwealth from the map. Poland would not be seen again until it was recreated in the aftermath of World War I.

Through these actions, the Russian Empire gained control of the lands that today comprise modern Belarus and the Jewish population that had settled in this region. The Russians felt concerned by the number of Jews now residing within the borders of the empire. To prevent them from extending any economic or religious influence deeper into Russia, Czar Nicholas I created the Pale of Settlement. This limited the right of residency for Jews to a wide strip of land along the western border of the Russian Empire. The Pale of Settlement included much of the territory of modern Ukraine, Lithuania, Moldova, and all of Belarus. It was here that the Jewish shtetl culture, made famous by the book, film, and musical *Fiddler on the Roof,* developed.

However, antisemitic tendencies within Russia grew, and violent attacks on Jewish communities, known as pogroms, began. These were often inspired by institutionalized, anti-Jewish sentiments from the Russian Orthodox Church including the 1903 Kishinev pogrom in Moldova, which Orthodox priests led immediately after concluding their Easter services. Antisemitic publications printed in Russia accusing the Jews of a plot to take over the world only added to the fervor. *The Protocols of the Elders of Zion* became the most famous version of this conspiracy theory. It was a counterfeit document that claimed to describe the Jews' dastardly plans for world domination. The false accusations of the *Protocols* were widely published, even reaching America, where Henry Ford, founder of the Ford Motor Company, distributed it through his newspaper, *The Dearborn Independent.*

Once again, the Jewish people of Eastern Europe found themselves facing the threat of violence. Many began looking for a new way of escape, and America became a Promised Land for some. Others increased their support for Zionism, with the goal of creating a Jewish homeland in Israel.

The most violent pogroms were in the Ukraine and Moldova regions of the Russian Empire, while Belarusian territory saw a smaller-scale outbreak of anti-Jewish violence in 1905–1906.[2]

Russia's defeat in World War I and the Communist Revolution led to the end of the Russian Empire and the birth of the Soviet Union.

In the aftermath of World War I, the first effort to create an independent Belarus took place. In March 1918, as the war neared its end, the new Soviet government signed a peace treaty, surrendering control of Belarusian territory to Germany. With the support of the occupying German army, an independent Belarusian People's Republic was founded. Its existence was short lived, as the Germans surrendered to the Western allies and withdrew their troops from Belarus. The Soviets swept in and created the Socialist Soviet Republic of Belarus (Belarusian SSR), part of the USSR.

For Jewish people who did not immigrate to other countries, the Bolshevik Revolution in 1918 and the rise of Communism, with its promises of equality, seemed to offer some hope. After Belarus became part of the USSR, the Soviets appointed a Jewish military officer named Yan Gamarnik as the first supreme commissar of Belarus. The Soviets initially recognized all the major ethnic groups in Belarus. They even included the state motto, written in Yiddish (the language of Ashkenazi Jewry), on the national seal alongside Russian, Belarusian, and Polish.

The emblem of the Belarusian Soviet Socialist Republic with the national motto in Russian, Belarusian, Polish, and Yiddish

By the 1930s, the Jewish population of Belarus decreased due to continued immigration to the United States. Still, the Soviet Union had the second-highest Jewish population in Europe with most Soviet Jews living in

7

the Pale of Settlement that spanned Belarus and Ukraine. It is estimated that 6–8 percent of Belarus was Jewish. In the cities, the number was much higher. Census data from a few decades before estimates the urban population was 30–74 percent Jewish. With such a large Jewish population, it is not surprising that Belarus was the birthplace of several famous Jewish figures. These include the Alter Rebbe, founder of the Orthodox Hasidic Chabad-Lubavitch movement, the artist Marc Chagall, and Eliezer Ben-Yehuda, the linguist who revived Hebrew as a modern spoken language. Jewish political figures including Chaim Weizmann, the man who secured the Balfour Declaration from the British and later served as the first president of Israel, and several prime ministers of Israel, including Shimon Peres and Menachem Begin, were also born on Belarusian soil.

September 1, 1939 is the date that most historians agree marks the beginning of World War II with the Nazi German invasion of Poland. While France and Great Britain quickly condemned the Nazi aggression and declared war on Hitler, the Soviets did not respond to Hitler's actions. Only a week before the Nazis attacked Poland, the foreign minister of the Soviet Union, Vyacheslav Molotov, hosted his German counterpart, Joachim von Ribbentrop, in Moscow. They signed a treaty of nonaggression, committing to a promise that neither nation would carry out hostile action against the other.

In addition to signing the official pact, Ribbentrop personally met with Joseph Stalin, the leader of the Soviet Union, and developed a secret plan to divide the other countries of northeastern Europe between them. Under this secret agreement, Poland would once again be partitioned. A week later, the Nazi Wehrmacht (German armed forces) struck Poland in a surprise attack.

Shortly after the Germans invaded Poland, Stalin sent Russian troops to seize eastern Poland and annex this territory to the Belarusian SSR. With this action, several hundred thousand more Jews found themselves within the borders of Belarus. This number grew with refugees fleeing German-occupied western Poland. By 1941, the Jewish population living within the expanded Belarusian borders more than doubled with estimates of 690,000 to 1,000,000.[3]

The peaceful Jewish life in Belarus was about to change dramatically.

CHAPTER 2

Like Lightning: The War Begins

The chariots storm through the streets,
rushing back and forth through the squares.
They look like flaming torches; they dart about like lightning.
—Nahum 2:4[4]

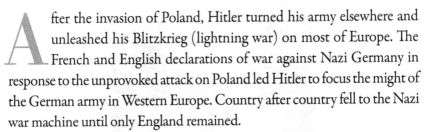

Afeter the invasion of Poland, Hitler turned his army elsewhere and unleashed his Blitzkrieg (lightning war) on most of Europe. The French and English declarations of war against Nazi Germany in response to the unprovoked attack on Poland led Hitler to focus the might of the German army in Western Europe. Country after country fell to the Nazi war machine until only England remained.

From September 1939 to the summer of 1941, the Soviets lived without much concern for Hitler. With the assurance of the Molotov-Ribbentrop Pact, it seemed they had nothing to worry about.

Little did they know that Hitler was drawing up a plan code named Operation Barbarossa to launch a surprise invasion of the Soviet Union. The Nazis massed three million soldiers and six hundred thousand vehicles on the Soviet border. Troops from Romania, Finland, Hungary, Italy, and Croatia joined the German Wehrmacht on the Soviet border. More than four thousand planes of the Luftwaffe (air force) stood by, and some began to fly over Soviet positions on reconnaissance missions.

The Soviet high command became concerned by the Nazi actions but did not think an invasion was possible. In addition to the nonaggression pact, Germany was still fighting England and surely would not want a two-front war.

Yaakov

However, some who were aware of the buildup took precautions. One person who realized the danger was a Jewish soldier named Lazar Levin. Lazar was an assistant commander of a Soviet communication division stationed in the city of Grodno on the western Belarusian border with German-occupied Poland. His young wife, Vera Kobrina, and sons, six-year-old Yaakov and four-year-old Mikhail (Misha), lived there with him. Knowing of the possible German threat, Lazar informed his wife that if war broke out, there was a plan to evacuate the families of military officers. He instructed her to take the boys to the front gate of the base if anything happened, and a car would be waiting there for them.

Yaakov

Early Sunday morning, June 22, 1941, the German Blitzkrieg began. Surprised Soviet positions came under intense artillery and aerial bombardment that was quickly followed by advancing German infantry and Panzers (tanks).

Seeing Grodno under attack, Vera gathered her sons and rushed to the gate. They found everything in a state of confusion and the car they were supposed to ride in already filled. They watched helplessly as it drove away.

After waiting for about twenty minutes, the young family found space in another car, and they set out. This delay probably saved their lives. The car that left before them took a direct hit from a bomb and was blown to pieces. They stopped and attempted to help the wounded survivors before being forced to take shelter from the continuing bombardment. Miraculously, their car was undamaged, and they continued their escape to Minsk.

Leonid

Despite the war on the border, all was quiet in the capital city of Minsk on June 22. In fact, there was great excitement, because the inauguration ceremony opening Lake Komsomolskaya was planned for later in the day. Leonid Rubenstein, a Jewish boy who had just finished seventh grade, was particularly excited. He and his schoolmates had taken part in digging the lake for their physical education class. Looking forward to a swim in the new lake to start the summer break, Leonid and several friends snuck out of their homes early that morning, planning to enjoy the cool water.

When they arrived, they found a crowd had gathered but no festivities. As soon as they joined the crowd, they heard about the Nazi attack. Leonid remembered listening to the radio as Molotov (the foreign minister who signed the secret pact with the Nazis a few years before) spoke of the surprise German attack and encouraged the Soviet people to prepare for a Great Patriotic War to defend the motherland.

Leonid and his friends headed home, chatting about how it was such a pity that the war would not last long enough for them to fight in it. Surely Germany would soon be defeated, and life would return to normal. While Leonid lamented his inability to go to war, others prepared to answer Molotov's call to arms.

Lev

For Lev Gurevich, the surge of patriotism and the threat that the Soviet Union faced swept away his prewar plans. Lev was born in Tatarsk, a shtetl in Russia's Smolensk region next to the Belarusian border. His father, Simeon, worked as a shoemaker but dreamed of providing a better life and education for his children. Realizing they could not obtain this in the shtetl, Simeon and Etta moved to the nearby city of Yartsevo with their children. Lev graduated from high school in 1936, having proved to be an excellent student. Because of his grades, he could attend any university he preferred. As he considered his options, he realized that his family needed assistance. His elder sister Gita was ill, and he chose to delay his studies to stay home and help earn money for the family to live. He found a job as a math and physics teacher, and after a year of helping his family, he began studying at Moscow State Pedagogical Institute. On June 21, 1941, he fulfilled his father's dream for him to get a good education as he graduated from university.

The next day, the Nazis invaded, and Lev's dreams for the future were postponed again. He hurried to the enlistment office to volunteer to fight and then heard Stalin's call for the reactivation of the People's Militia. Lev and many of his friends who graduated with him chose to join the militia rather than the regular army. They received rifles, gas masks, and orders to go to the town of Roslavl near the Belarusian border to prepare defenses against the German Blitzkrieg.

The Nazis called their war strategy Blitzkrieg because they struck hard and fast and would overrun huge amounts of territory in days if not hours. Lev was stationed on the Belarusian border with Russia because the Soviets had already lost much of Belarus. The Red Army was weak due to purges Stalin had carried out in the 1930s. Over several years, he had executed many experienced military commanders when he perceived them to be a threat to his power. When the German attack came, the Soviet forces were unprepared because of the lack of experienced leadership and rapidly lost ground.

The Germans gained air superiority within hours, destroying much of the Soviet Air Force on the ground. They were so successful that when reports reached Berlin about the damage to the Soviet aircraft, Hermann Göring, supreme commander of the Luftwaffe, was skeptical and ordered the reports to be checked. It turned out the original numbers that he found unbelievable were conservative and even more of the Soviet Air Force had been destroyed.

Leonid

The day after his trip to the lake when he found out about the war, Leonid met his friends, and they began discussing the war. A plane flew overhead. One friend said it was the Soviet Air Force, and another said it was not. Everyone looked up, saw the cross on the wings, and realized it was a

German reconnaissance plane. Leonid remembered the surreal feeling of seeing a German plane over Minsk. However, the quiet did not last long. The next planes were not unarmed reconnaissance planes but German bombers. Leonid and his family lived near the government building in the center of Minsk, which was targeted. A bomb blew out their windows, and a piece of shrapnel struck Leonid in the leg. The family rushed to the bomb shelter in the school and waited. Wave after wave of bombers struck. The Germans bombed Minsk eleven times that day. When the bombing ended in the evening, they emerged to find their city in flames. Survivors described how it looked like daylight because the fires burned so brightly that night.

Minsk in flames after the bombing

Yaakov

This was the condition of Minsk when six-year-old Yaakov Levin arrived with his mother and brother. They were in the car that evacuated them from the front lines where his father, Lazar, served. However, their evacuation ended in Minsk. The railroad had been bombed, and there was no way to continue. They were not the only people to arrive. Refugees flooded into Minsk, hoping for safety and leadership in the capital. However, Panteleimon Ponomarenko, the first secretary of the central committee of the Communist Party of Belarus, fled to Moscow, leaving the people of the city to their fate. The militia patrolled the streets for a day to maintain order and prevent looting, and then they disappeared. The leadership evacuated without making efforts to help or warn the general population, a fact that led many to feel that they had been forsaken. Minsk was left without any governing structure or order, and looting began. Everyone was terrified and confused in the ensuing chaos.

Yaakov's mother, Vera, decided not to stay in Minsk, and she set out on foot with her two boys. They were accompanied by a friend with her one-year-old daughter. Vera headed for the city of Babruysk, which was more than 150 km farther east. Babruysk was Lazar's hometown, and Vera hoped her in-laws would be able to help them. Yaakov could walk, but the other two children were too young to do so, so his mother and her friend carried them.

As they left Minsk, horrible sights lined the road and seared themselves in the six-year-old's memory. The Nazis' air superiority allowed them to carry out airstrikes on the fleeing troops and refugees. The family passed lone children without anyone to care for them and bodies scattered along the road. They bought food in villages they passed through until their money ran out. The children began crying from hunger and fear. They saw some dead soldiers near a van, which was full of bags of hard biscuits. Vera examined the bags and saw a warning written on them: Do not touch! It is poisoned! She took some biscuits just in case, and they continued. Eventually, Vera became so exhausted that she hardly had the strength to carry her son, Misha. Misha was silent, too weak to even cry any longer.

Some mothers, driven by desperation, left their children at strangers' doors, hoping that someone would care for them. Others were in such despair that they committed suicide. After the Levin's money ran out, they became so hungry that Vera risked feeding the children the "poisoned" biscuits. Thankfully, the warning must have been meant to prevent theft, since no one suffered any ill effects from them.

Despite their exhaustion, Yaakov, Vera, Misha, and their friends found the strength to continue. It took them more than a week to reach Babruysk.

When they arrived, the German army was already there. They found empty, looted apartments where their relatives once lived. Brokenhearted and exhausted, they moved into an empty apartment. The stores had been looted, and they could not find any food. Vera's plan to find relatives had failed, and they faced an incredibly desperate situation without food or safe shelter. Vera heard that there was still syrup in a nearby candy factory, so she took Yaakov and set out to get some. Crowds were waiting in lines to get to the tanks of syrup. After waiting for hours, they reached the tank only to find the body of a man who had drowned in the syrup. The desperate people did not let the body prevent them from getting something to eat, and they continued collecting syrup around it.

Such desperation spread across Belarus as the Nazis swiftly occupied the country. It took the German army about a month to occupy all of Belarus. The invasions started on June 22, and by July 26, they entered Mogilev, not far from the Belarussian border with Russia. In every city and countless villages across Belarus, German soldiers suddenly appeared.

Alexander

The Germans' arrival changed Alexander Mysov's world in one afternoon. Alexander was born in the city of Mogilev, and when the war began, he was a sixteen-year-old living with his parents, Georgy Mysov and Maria Dmitrievna, and his sisters Zoya, Tamara, and Larisa. The family loved music, and his parents even sang in a choir at the local church.

Alexander with Zoya and Tamara

15

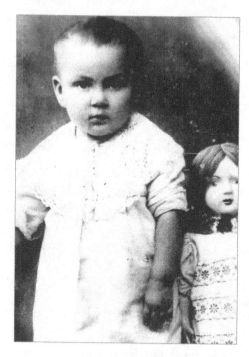

Little sister Larisa

Mogilev amateur choir in 1939. Alexander Mysov (first row, third from left), his mother, Maria (second row, second from left), and his sister, Zoya (second row, fourth from left)

Alexander's love for music led him to study at the music college where he played the violin in the orchestra. He did not let the news of the war affect his commitment to the orchestra and continued to attend rehearsals. One day, on his way home, his cousin rushed to meet him, shouting frantically. He explained to Alexander that the Nazis were at his house. However, these were no ordinary German soldiers. Many of the combat soldiers passed by, and although they stole food, they did not otherwise bother civilians. These troops at Alexander's house were members of a special Nazi task force, the Einsatzgruppen. A neighbor had told them that his family was Jewish, and the Nazis surrounded the house with dogs and arrested his entire family. In addition to this horrifying news, his cousin warned that the neighbor had reported Alexander as well, and now the Nazis were looking for him.

Alexander realized that he had no home to return to and had lost his entire beloved family. However, he had no time to grieve. The members of the Einsatzgruppe that captured his family began searching the area with their dogs and calling his name. With the Nazis' voices and dogs' barking ringing in his ears, he ran for his life and swam across the Dnieper River to throw the dogs off his scent.

During the invasion of the USSR, the Nazis created special task forces called Einsatzgruppen that operated in Belarus and Ukraine. Their task was to advance behind the Wehrmacht and hunt down "threats." They targeted Jews and Communist Party members. Their brutal campaign was the beginning of their large-scale murder of Jews. The Einsatzgruppe arrived in a village with a Jewish population and forcibly recruited non-Jewish locals (often including children) to dig mass graves at the outskirts of the town. Then they would gather the Jewish people while their neighbors watched helplessly, march them to the freshly dug grave, and shoot them. Locals would sometimes be forced to return to fill in the hole and sort the clothing of the victims, and then the Einsatzgruppe would move on to the next village. Local witnesses described how the earth covering these graves convulsed for as long as two days as the wounded struggled under the mass of bodies and dirt before they died. This early phase of the Holocaust is referred to as "the Holocaust by bullets" as it did not rely on centralized killing centers such as Auschwitz that we often associate with the Holocaust. The Einsatzgruppen left few signs of the horrors they committed: only a mass grave, scattered bullet casings, and the stunned witnesses who had helplessly watched the murder of their Jewish neighbors.[5]

Only later would Alexander learn his family's fate. The Einsatzgruppe took them to Polykovichi, a village they chose to dispose of the Jewish people from the region of Mogilev. There, like many other Jewish victims, they were killed and buried in the mass graves that had been prepared for the waves of victims from the surrounding area.

Alexander's only refuge was the vast Belarusian countryside. However, many others thought that the cities would provide more safety and fled into them.

Sima

Thirteen-year-old Sima Margolina lived in the village of Uzda, southwest of Minsk, on a farm with her family. More than three hundred Jewish families lived in Uzda, making up about 33 percent of the village. Sima's family consisted of her parents, Mendel Berkovich and Ella Abramovna, and her younger sisters: Nechama, who had just finished third grade and was smart and active, and five-year-old Berta, who the older girls often cared for. The family raised chickens, geese, and a cow. They also grew vegetables and lived a simple and happy life. When the Nazi troops arrived in their small village, everything changed. Sima's parents knew it was dangerous to be Jewish in an area under Nazi control. Her father joined the partisans to fight the Nazis and began living in the forest. Her mother took the children and headed toward Minsk, believing they would be safe in the capital. A short time after her family left Uzda, the Einsatzgruppe arrived on motorcycles. The remaining Jewish people of Uzda were loaded onto trucks, taken into the woods, and shot.

Sima's family escaped this fate by leaving their farm and everything they owned behind and walking 70 km (43 miles) to Minsk. The roads were packed with refugees, and in the confused, fearful, and shocked crowds, Sima, Nechama, and Berta became separated from their mother. The girls carried on by themselves and reached Minsk, but the situation there had gotten much worse. The bombing, burning buildings, and chaos of a city without leadership that Leonid witnessed in the opening days of the war was only the beginning of the horrors that would descend upon Minsk.

Leonid

While others fled, Leonid's family stayed in Minsk. His grandmother convinced his family that they did not need to worry or evacuate. She spoke of how German soldiers had come to Minsk during World War I. She assured everyone that the Germans had been normal, decent people the last time they occupied the city. They did not harm civilians and overall acted in a civilized manner. She insisted they should not fear the Germans, and this convinced Leonid's parents to stay. Many people likely recalled the role Germany played in establishing the first Belarusian Republic, when Belarus gained independence for the first time in its history. If they had only known how radically different this occupation would be, of course, they would have joined the panicked crowds flooding out of the city.

The Nazis arrived in Minsk on June 28, a week after the invasion began. They covered the 275 km (170 miles) in a few days since there was only isolated resistance. After marching into Minsk in grand style, the Germans began restoring order and shooting looters on sight.

The Nazis proclaimed themselves the liberators of the Belarusian people. Leonid recalled the signs they plastered across the city declaring that they had come to deliver the people from the oppression of the "Jewish Communists." A central part of Nazi ideology and propaganda suggested that Communism was a Jewish plot to control the world. The fact that many Jewish thinkers and revolutionaries supported the Communist Revolution offered "proof" of these claims. In reality, most Jews were not Communists, and religious Jews often faced persecution by the Soviet government.

Soon after arriving, the Nazis gathered all the men ages fifteen to forty-five and took them to an improvised prison camp they created in the village of Drozdy just outside of Minsk. The soldiers roped off a section of swampy ground beside the river and placed armed guards around it. Here the men of Minsk sat and waited for the Nazis to identify Communist Party members and Jews. The Nazis released the Belarusian civilians who they did not consider a threat. However, for the Jewish people and card-carrying Communists, the detainment continued. They waited for days without food, water, or shelter. Many women came to visit their husbands and bring them food when they discovered where they had been taken. Twelve-year-old Zoya Oboz remembers visiting Drozdy with her mother to bring food to her father.

Zoya

In the happier times before the war, Zoya lived in a three-room apartment in Minsk with her parents, Rebekah and Yaakov, her grandparents, her sisters Faina and Ira, and her brother, Isaac. She remembers her grandmother baking matzah, the unleavened bread traditionally eaten on Passover, and her mother's reputation for hospitality in their community. She grew up in an Orthodox Jewish family and remembers how her grandfather attended synagogue. Her father and grandfather worked as skilled carpenters and cabinetmakers. She remembers her father's strict discipline in response to the mischief she and her siblings often got into and his ability to silence them with a glare. She and her brother mimicked their father's habit of heavy smoking by making cigarettes out of the newspaper and pretending to smoke. However, one day, this game lost its appeal when after lighting his newspaper "cigarette," her brother burned his lips. Still, Zoya was a wild and spunky child who often took risks. Once she was almost hit by a tram when she jumped in front of it to win a bet. Fortunately, the driver stopped just in time and avoided a disaster.

When the Nazis invaded, Zoya's family tried to escape but were unable to, and they were forced to return to Minsk. Back in their house, Zoya and the other children watched from the attic as the Nazis began rounding up the men and boys. Soon they reached her house and took her father to Drozdy. Her mother packed a basket of food and cigarettes and took Zoya to deliver it to him there. They found the men surrounded by heavy German security, sitting on the open ground without any shelter. They were allowed to pass the basket over the rope, but they were unsure if anything would be left in it by the time it reached her father.

After a few days, the Nazis identified and separated more than three thousand Jewish men in Drozdy who admitted to having a higher education. Some hoped that their qualifications would prove their value.

However, with the exceptions of doctors, engineers, and those with advanced training that would be useful, all the intelligentsia were taken away and shot. Zoya's father's valuable skill as a builder led to his release. However, his freedom was short lived, as the whole family soon faced confinement in the ghetto.

CHAPTER 3

Surrounded by Squalor and Suffering: The Ghettos

L ess than a month after the Nazis arrived, posters from the new German Reichskommissariat Ostland (Reich Commissioner of the Eastern Land) appeared on July 20, informing the population of Minsk that a Jewish neighborhood was being created. In conjunction with this order, the Nazis created the Judenrat (Jewish Council), comprised of Jewish citizens to whom they allocated much of the responsibility of governing Jewish affairs. They would oversee the movement of the Jewish population to the ghetto and create lists of all Jews for the Nazis' use.

The Nazis gave everyone five days to move, and the newly formed Judenrat had to collect and pay the huge sum of 300,000 rubles to the Nazi administration to cover the cost of this relocation.

All Belarusian inhabitants in a central part of the city were forced to relocate to make room for the Jewish population. This area would be the Minsk Ghetto, the new "home" of the Jewish people of Minsk.

The Minsk Ghetto with a warning sign that anyone trying to climb the fence would be shot

The Nazis created 228 ghettos in Belarus alone and more than 1,100 in Central and Eastern Europe. Each ghetto functioned like a miniature concentration camp, set up in neighborhoods where families once lived in peace. Minsk became the largest ghetto in the Soviet Union and the fourth largest in Europe with more than one hundred thousand Jewish men, women, and children. They found themselves confined in their new neighborhood by tall, barbed wire fences.

The Nazis previously implemented the idea of confining the Jews to ghettos in Poland where the largest ghettos of the Holocaust, including Lodz and Warsaw, stood. However, the Nazis did not create the concept of the ghetto. The Jewish people often experienced living in ghettos throughout European history. In 1516, the Republic of Venice created the first ghetto, requiring the city's Jews to live in one particular neighborhood. In 1555, Pope Paul IV issued a papal bull *cum nimis absurdum,* declaring the need to confine Jews to a ghetto to prevent them from mixing with the Christian population. Christian Europe based the ghetto on the idea that Jewish differences meant they should be separated from the rest of society, sometimes out of discrimination and sometimes to protect them from a hostile public. However, the Nazis' reinvention of the ghetto proved far more brutal than any previously seen in Europe.

When one thinks of the Holocaust, images of the horrible reality of gas chambers and concentration camps often come to mind. However, an often-overlooked fact is that the Holocaust developed as the Nazis invented and experimented with different methods of persecuting and murdering Jewish people. Their efforts to persecute Jews demonstrated a clear progression with each new policy representing a more radical type of persecution. These ghettos represent a key stage of the Holocaust.

When the Nazis invaded the Soviet Union in 1941, the infamous plan that would be labeled "the final solution to the Jewish question" was still developing. The question of what to do with the Jewish people still seemed to be in the Nazis' minds. In the early days of the Nazi regime, Hitler's goals included stripping German Jews of their citizenship and driving them out of Germany, thus making Germany "Judenrein" (cleansed of Jews). Now, after the Nazis occupied so many other countries in Europe, driving the Jews away no longer seemed possible. Many German Jews had resettled in other European countries when they had been forced to leave Germany. They thought they had escaped Hitler, only to see the countries they had sought refuge in fall into Nazi hands as the Blitzkrieg swept across Europe. Anne Frank and her family are a classic example of this, having left their Frankfurt home to flee across the Dutch border to perceived safety in Amsterdam. The Nazis considered plans for mass deportations to Madagascar or Palestine to get the Jews out of Europe. Göring, one of Hitler's closest associates, instructed Reinhard Heydrich, the head of the SD (Nazi secret police) to prepare to "solve the Jewish question by emigration and evacuation in the most favorable way possible, given present conditions."[6] The "present conditions" of war with England and Germany's lack of a strong navy would make deporting the Jewish population impossible. While the Nazis plotted, the ghettos served as a useful tool that allowed them to control and isolate the Jewish population. It made it easier to enslave, humiliate, abuse, rob, torture, starve, and ultimately murder them.

The ghettos also provided slave labor. Slavery might not be a word that is often associated with the Holocaust, but it played an intricate part in the Nazi persecution of the Jewish people. The first order the Nazis issued to create a ghetto in Lodz, Poland, made it clear that the ghetto would be a temporary answer to the Jewish question and enable the creation of a slave force of able-bodied Jews as "labor battalions."

In January 1942, at the Wannsee Conference near Berlin, Heydrich presented a different plan for the "total solution" of "the Jewish question." Here the Nazis found their diabolical final answer to the Jewish question: a plan to annihilate Europe's Jews in one of the greatest acts of mass murder in history.

Meanwhile, in the ghettos, the Jewish residents were unaware of the gathering horror. As they occupied their new "homes," they hoped that this time of persecution would soon pass. In Minsk, the Nazis surrounded the ghetto with a high barbed wire fence. Unlike in Poland where they surrounded the ghettos with a cement or brick wall, here only the barbed wire stood between the ghetto and freedom. Although the people did not know it then, the less-secure fence played a role in saving countless lives in the later stages of the ghetto's existence.

By August 1, 1941, just eleven days after the order creating the ghetto, more than eighty thousand Jewish men, women, and children had been packed into a small area of the city where they awaited their fate.

As they hastily packed a few belongings and headed to the ghetto, they rushed to find a place to live. Families attempted to find relatives to live with and empty apartments they could occupy. The Nazis allotted 1 1/2 square meters of living space per person (a little more than 16 square feet). To put this in context, the average one-bedroom apartment in the United States today is about 880 square feet. If the average one-bedroom American apartment was in the Minsk ghetto, more than forty people would have been required to live in it. Needless to say, the prisoners in the ghetto faced terrible overcrowding.

Almost all the Jewish people in Minsk, including Zoya, Sima, and Leonid, ended up in the ghetto. Zoya and her family moved into her uncle's apartment. Soon more than twenty family members packed into their two-room flat.

Leonid

Leonid's family exchanged their home with a Belarusian who lived in the ghetto territory, and soon twenty to twenty-five members of their extended family moved in with them. The only space Leonid could find to sleep in the crowded apartment was under the table in the kitchen.

Sima

Sima arrived in Minsk with her two little sisters after walking 70 km (43 miles) from her village only to be sent to the ghetto. There, the girls found their mother, who had been separated from them on the journey.

They faced appalling conditions. Without electricity or firewood, people were unable to cook or heat their houses. The Nazis gave rations to the Judenrat for the ghetto population, but it was never enough to go around. Most of the food the Nazis supplied was given only to those who worked for them, and the small rations they received had to be brought home and shared with their families, who received no other food. People hunted for firewood and food everywhere. The winter of 1941 was particularly harsh, and as it set in, people got even more desperate. Sima's family burned books and furniture in a vain effort to stay warm. People tore down fences and ripped boards off houses to use as firewood.

Leonid

For people on the brink of starvation, finding food became the constant focus of their days. Leonid's grandmother instructed him to go out and collect raspberry leaves from the bushes in people's yards. As he stripped the leaves off the bushes he could find, he wondered what his grandmother wanted the leaves for. He didn't realize that raspberry leaf tea was a traditional folk remedy for various health issues and full of nutrients, which was exactly why his grandmother wanted them. She hung the leaves up to dry in their crowded apartment to ensure the family would have at least a small supply of nutrients in the days ahead.

Zoya

Zoya's uncle escaped Minsk, so his apartment was empty when Zoya's family moved in. The apartment was near the mosque of the Tatar community that settled in Belarus due to the Mongol invasions of the Middle Ages. Next to the mosque was a garden, and her family often snuck into it to steal vegetables. They risked being shot, but the fresh vegetables supplied them with lifesaving nutrition. Another risky way to get food was to trade with local Belarusians who brought food to the fence surrounding the ghetto and offered to trade it for clothing or valuables. This practice could be dangerous as it was technically forbidden. However, for those inside the ghetto, a meal was worth the risk. Zoya's family traded to get flour or bread over the fence. This was not enough, so they resorted to collecting grass and food scraps from the trash. Zoya remembers how she was so hungry that grass soup tasted delicious to her.

When they learned the Nazis would give some food to workers, everyone who was physically able tried to get work. As a little twelve-year-old girl, Zoya got a job helping to clean the streets, removing rubble left by the bombing. She spent her days moving heavy bricks and rubble for about half a loaf (150 grams or 5 ounces) of bread a day. This meager portion was insufficient nourishment for someone doing hard physical labor all day. However, most laborers had families who could not work, and they brought their food home to share. To make matters worse, the Nazis often mixed sawdust with the flour to stretch it further, but of course this added no nutrients or other benefits for the starving people. The work was incredibly hard, especially for children. Zoya remembers how one day, as they were struggling to gather heavy bricks, her mother stopped working and looked sadly at her children. Noticing that she had paused her work, one of the guards struck her mother with a whip, leaving a large scar on her back. Zoya cried for the rest of the day after witnessing her mother being whipped.

Only those too young or too old to work were constantly imprisoned in the ghetto, as the Nazis exploited anyone they could as slave labor. First in the ghettos and then in concentration camps, they selected those who were able to work and forced them to slave away under terrible conditions for the benefit of the Nazi Reich. In the ghetto, work details were gathered and marched under guard each morning to wherever they had been assigned to work. The Nazis wanted to wring every ounce of energy and manpower that they could out of these poor people, reduced to slavery in the twentieth century, before murdering them.

Leonid

Often laborers who worked in factories risked their lives to steal Nazi supplies. They saw this as both an act of revenge against the Nazis and a way to get valuable goods to trade for food on the black market. Like every effort to get food, this came with the risk of being tortured and shot if caught. Leonid and his father had been assigned to a painting crew, and once the Nazis gave them cooking oil to make into drying oil that they needed for the paint. His father and the other workers carefully poured off a little of the oil, since it was valuable in the ghetto. The next day, the Nazi guards noticed there seemed to be less oil and beat the crew to force them to confess to stealing it. Although Leonid was spared a beating, his father and the others could barely walk home that night.

Sometimes workers received food from sympathetic passersby or even German civilian workers who had moved to Minsk to manage the factories and the Jewish slave labor force. Often, when marching to work, the ragged, emaciated Jews saw other residents of Minsk going about their daily lives in relative peace. They saw people dressed up and going to the movies and a night out on the town, sights that made them long even more for a return to normal life.

Not only were deprivation, persecution, and starvation taking their toll on the people, but overpopulation led to outbreaks of all sorts of diseases. Many people did not have indoor plumbing, and the overworked, malnourished people packed into the ghetto became the perfect breeding ground for germs.

Irina

The horrible conditions the Nazis subjected them to are forever seared into their memories. For two-year-old Irina Sussman, the most memorable aspect of her ordeal was the smell and filth.

Faina Sussman

David Sussman (in center)

Irina lived in Minsk with her parents, David and Faina Sussman, and older siblings Anatoly, Heinrich, and Alla. Her family was forced to leave their home and were herded into the ghetto where the sights and smells were beyond imagination. The stench of rotting flesh and filth hung in the air. This horrid smell of death served as a constant reminder of the ever-present threat of an untimely end. Irina experienced this horrible reality far too soon when her father disappeared while out looking for food. Almost everyone in the ghetto experienced the pain of not being able to say goodbye or even knowing what exactly happened to loved ones who disappeared. Despite losing her husband, Faina tried to carry on, struggling to protect and provide for her children. The young widow would leave Irina's seven-year-old brother, Heinrich, to care for his little sisters while she went to look for food. Anatoly, the oldest, had been at a summer camp when the war began and was evacuated to safety. One day, their mother did not return. The starving, ill, terrified children waited for her and wept for days. Relatives and friends tried to do what they could, but they could offer little comfort.

If the horror of starvation, brutality, sickness, and cold was not enough, the Nazis brought a new terror. The Nazis called them *Aktionen* (actions in German), but those in the ghetto referred to them as pogroms.

By November 7, 1941, one month before the "Day of Infamy" when America entered World War II after the attack on Pearl Harbor, the prisoners in the Minsk Ghetto had already survived three months of horrible suffering. It did not look like the war would end anytime soon, since the German army was on the outskirts of the great Soviet cities of Leningrad (modern-day St. Petersburg) and Moscow. The seventh marked the twenty-fourth anniversary of the Communist Revolution, a national holiday. In Moscow, Stalin spoke to the Red Army troops preparing to deploy to the front lines. He spoke of the just war and task of liberation that had fallen into the hands of the Red Army and reminded them how occupied Europe waited to be liberated from Nazi occupation.

Leonid

Leonid recalled how his grandmother, trying to keep the family's spirits up, prepared to celebrate with a holiday dinner. Due to their conditions, the holiday "feast" consisted of a spoonful of mashed herring and potato peels per person.

Meanwhile, the Nazis took the opportunity to observe the holiday in their own twisted way. They took the columns of workers out of the ghetto for their daily work. This meant only those who could not work—the elderly, the ill, and children—remained inside the ghetto. Soldiers and Polizei swept into the southernmost section of the ghetto and went door to door, ordering everyone into the street. The Polizei who participated in this Aktion were collaborators who served in auxiliary police units and assisted in the Nazi crimes. In Belarus, the Polizei units consisted of Ukrainians, Lithuanians, and local Belarusians.[7]

The Aktion filled the ghetto with the shouting of soldiers mingled with the screams of terrified people, barking dogs, and shots. People in other parts of the ghetto did not know what was happening and remained hidden indoors. Those in the section under attack tried to hide. By the end of the day, the Nazis and their collaborators marched between twelve thousand and seventeen thousand people out of the ghetto to a village nearby called Turchynka. They forced the people to undress, and the Nazi Einsatzgruppe A and Ukrainian police units stepped forward to shoot them. The bodies were buried in mass graves like so many other victims of the Einsatzgruppen.

The Nazis described this Aktion as an anti-Communist operation in an attempt to associate the Jews with the Communists, even forcing the Jews to carry banners celebrating the revolution as they marched away to their deaths.

Zoya

On November 20, the Nazis returned and carried out a second Aktion to clear a section from Zamkovaya Street to Podzamkovoya Street of all Jewish residents. That morning, Zoya got up at 5:00 a.m. to go to work with her father in the Belarusian section of the city outside the ghetto. Nazis began coming down the street, pounding on doors and windows and ordering people into the street. They divided everyone into two columns with able-bodied workers on one side and the elderly and children on the other. Zoya's immediate family was placed in the column of workers, but she saw her grandparents separated into the other column and taken away. That was the last time Zoya saw her beloved grandparents. She later learned they were among six thousand to seven thousand Jews taken to Turchynka that day to be shot.

The Nazis intended to gradually reduce the size of the ghetto and empty whole streets of residents while murdering those who served no practical use to them. They deliberately carried out these Aktionen at times when the majority of the workers were outside the ghetto, so they knew only the weak, elderly, ill, and children remained to be murdered. When Zoya's family returned from work, they found someone else living in their apartment and thus needed to find a new place to live. They eventually found a rat-infested house in another part of the ghetto.

Leonid

Many people were forced to relocate to a new part of the ghetto due to the Aktionen. After the second Aktion, Leonid's distraught uncle and two cousins showed up at the family's door. They explained that four members of their family perished during the Aktion, and they did not know where to live. Leonid's grandmother instructed them to move into the already overcrowded apartment with the rest of the family.

In a matter of weeks that November, the Nazis slaughtered between eighteen thousand and twenty-four thousand Jewish men, women, and children. This number represented almost a quarter of the population of the ghetto.

Terror filled the ghetto after this brutal outbreak of extreme violence. The Aktionen threw the ghetto into greater chaos as people searched for family members and new places to live.

Anatoly

Twelve-year-old Anatoly Dikushin, who lived on Nemiga Street in the ghetto with his mother, was left homeless by the Aktion. His family moved to Minsk from Russia because his father, Mikhail, was an NKVD (Soviet secret police) agent. His mother, Serafima Crapchan, had grown up in a Jewish family in Minsk, and many of her relatives still lived there. When the war began, his non-Jewish father disappeared, probably due to his role as a Soviet secret agent, leaving Anatoly and his mother to fend for themselves. The Nazis threw them, along with Serafima's family, into the ghetto. Living in the Nemiga neighborhood (today a popular part of central Minsk) put them in the center of the first Aktion of 1941.

During the Aktion, Anatoly and his mother escaped and hid, thus avoiding the fate of being marched to their deaths. However, the pogrom left them homeless on the streets of the ghetto in November at the beginning of the worst winter Belarus had experienced in years. They probably would have frozen to death if a kind woman had not taken them in. In the aftermath of the Aktion, most people trapped in the ghetto were terrorized, never knowing when their captors would unleash another wave of murderous attacks. They lived in constant fear, expecting to be killed at any moment. Anatoly was an independent teenager and refused to give in to fear. He often went out and searched for food for himself and his mother near the railway station. The ghetto's streets were almost empty; all the able-bodied people were at work in factories, and those who remained behind hid to stay out of the Nazis' sight and avoid being murdered. Only children risked going out in the streets to search for food. Anatoly often went into houses where people had been murdered to try to find food or valuables to trade for food.

After "cleaning" part of the ghetto, the Nazis moved the fence. Some Belarusian families returned to the apartments whose previous residents lay buried in the mass graves in Turchynka. However, another reason for the Aktionen and emptying of parts of the ghetto soon became apparent. On one of his journeys to find food, Anatoly saw the Nemiga area where he used to live fenced off and turned into a second ghetto. A train loaded with German Jews from the city of Hamburg arrived. Then trains from cities across Germany, Austria, and Czechoslovakia began arriving in Minsk, each packed with Jewish men, women, and children. Residents of cities such as Cologne, Berlin, Bremen, and Vienna found themselves in Minsk. The Nazis informed them that although they could not live in Germany as Jews, they would be permitted to settle on the frontier of what Hitler anticipated would be the new Nazi Empire.

Once they arrived, they found themselves locked in a small ghetto in the center of Minsk, surrounded by a foreign culture and language. Although these "Hamburg Jews," as they we called, received some favorable treatment from the local Nazi government, they faced a huge challenge in not knowing Russian. This made it difficult to trade with the local population for food. Many Hamburg Jews owned much better clothing and jewelry than the poor Soviet Jews. Their rich appearance often impressed the Jews of Minsk, who thought they looked like movie stars. Despite this, they were still Jews, and thus their fate was no different than that of the poorer Soviet Jews. The Nazis created a ghetto within a ghetto and prohibited the Belarusian Jews and German Jews from mixing. Nevertheless, daring and desperate people conducted trades over the fence, and the German Jews found that many Belarusian Jews spoke Yiddish, enabling them to communicate a little. Yiddish is a Jewish language that developed in Germany in the Middle Ages and is somewhat intelligible to German speakers. However, the inability to speak Russian rendered the Hamburg Jews even more helpless than the Belarusian Jews. Without local connections or the ability to communicate, they did not have the assistance that the Belarusian Jews received from the resistance and local non-Jewish Belarusians who often helped their Jewish neighbors. For the Hamburg Jews, escape was almost impossible.

Leonid

The ghetto became a much scarier place after the Aktionen. Terror reigned as drunken German soldiers carried out raids with increasing frequency. They often drove into the ghetto in the middle of the night, randomly selecting a house to break into. They murdered the occupants and looted their belongings. No one knew if they would be awakened by a car stopping outside their door, bringing with it a sudden and violent death.

Whenever these night raids occurred, they left horrifying signs everywhere that made the crimes evident to every passerby the next morning. The sidewalk was often splattered with blood and brain matter and littered with cartridge casings and empty vodka bottles. Sometimes a cart sat nearby, filled with bodies and covered with a bloodstained sheet.

Leonid remembers the horror he experienced one day as he and his father helped remove bodies from a house that had been raided the night before. They found a pregnant woman who was stabbed in the stomach with a kitchen knife. Leonid could not comprehend how someone could be such a monster as to murder a pregnant woman.

Zoya

Despite the harsh winter, severe hunger, and lack of heat, along with almost nightly terror and murders, Sima, Leonid, Anatoly, Irina, and Zoya survived the winter of 1941–42 in the ghetto. However, Zoya lost her little brother, Isaac, who snuck out of the ghetto with one of their cousins to find food and never returned. The loss broke the hearts of the entire family, and Zoya remembers how her mother's sobs filled their apartment for days. Zoya now had not only lost her grandparents but also her closest friend and playmate. Only her parents and two sisters remained.

Leonid

The first of March marked six months of being imprisoned in the ghetto. Despite the unimaginable suffering, many refused to give up hope. Leonid recalls how his grandmother told the family that Purim was coming. The children did not understand what she meant and asked her to explain. She told them the Jewish holiday of Purim commemorated God's deliverance from a foreign power. She promised that one day, they would be free from the Nazis as well.

The story of Purim is found in the Tanakh (the Old Testament or Jewish Bible) in the Book of Esther. It celebrates Queen Esther's efforts to save the Jewish people living in exile in Persia from a plot to destroy them. In 1942, it fell on March 2. The Nazis seemed to have a morbid fascination with this holiday, often mentioning it in their antisemitic propaganda publications. They suggested that the Jews would like to reenact the events of the story, which ends with victory over their enemies. To the Nazis, this provided a twisted excuse to perceive themselves as victims, based on their assumption that the mostly defenseless Jews were looking for opportunities to kill Germans. The story of the Jews surviving an attempt to destroy them seemed to haunt some within the Nazi Party.

As Purim approached, the Nazis ordered the Judenrat to provide a special workforce of five thousand people. The Judenrat in Minsk used their authority over daily life in the ghetto to work closely with the underground, attempting to save their fellow Jews. Remembering how the first Aktion took place on the anniversary of the Communist Revolution, the Judenrat suspected the Nazis had other intentions for Purim and did not comply. Instead, they warned the people in the ghetto, and soon word spread that another Aktion may be in the works. This warning may have saved lives, but the refusal to cooperate with the Nazi demands cost the Judenrat members their lives, as the Nazis hung them in the aftermath of the Aktion they had foreseen.

People did everything they could to survive in the ghetto. After the November Aktionen, many people anticipated that more violence was yet to come and began creating hiding places called *malinas* (Russian for raspberry but used as a slang term for a hideout). This word sounded similar to the Hebrew *malon,* which means hotel, and thus it held a double meaning. Sometimes the malina was a basement or a room with a piece of furniture placed in such a way as to conceal the door. Others simply dug small holes under the floor or hollowed a space in a wall. Anywhere that someone could hide if the Nazis came became a malina.

However, the malinas offered only limited safety. Often people could not bring themselves to hide in the dark, cramped spaces for days and took their chances outside. The Nazis sometimes used dogs to search for people, and the malina was no match for a dog's nose. After discovering some malinas, the soldiers often threw grenades inside empty houses, expecting that another malina was located somewhere. Even if a malina was not discovered, it was still a dangerous place. Sometimes, while a family hid in the cramped darkness of their malina, listening to soldiers searching their house, a baby would start to cry. Attempting to stifle this noise that would endanger the entire family, mothers sometimes accidentally smothered their own children.

On March 2, the Nazis waited until the workers left and then viciously swept into the ghetto. This time, the Aktion was widespread and not solely focused on clearing a few streets. People scrambled into their malinas. The Nazis rounded up as many people as they could find and loaded them on trucks to be taken away and murdered.

At work with his father, Leonid did not know what was happening in the ghetto. When they returned, they saw an Aktion had taken place and rushed home only to find the house empty. Leonid panicked and began to scream, thinking his family had been taken away. In his panic, he forgot about the malina they had built under the floor of their porch. Suddenly, he heard the welcomed sound of familiar voices calling to him from the malina. After they climbed out, he heard the heartbreaking story of what happened.

When the Aktion began, his family hid in the malina. His grandmother waited until everyone got inside, covered it with boards, and placed the bucket they would use as a toilet on top of it. She knew that the horrible smell of the waste in the bucket would prevent the Nazis from spending much time searching the house, and that would increase the likelihood of her family not being found. Hiding in the malina, the family heard the Nazis enter the house and question her. She spoke some German and told them she was the only person at home. They heard the sounds of the Nazis beating her as she tried to plead and reason with them. They heard shots, followed by silence. Leonid's grandmother had sacrificed herself to protect her family.

The grieving family took her body to the *yama* (Russian for pit), an open mass grave in the ghetto where those killed in night raids or who died from starvation and illness could be buried.

The Yama Memorial to the victims of the Minsk Ghetto on the location where five thousand victims of the March 2 Purim pogrom were murdered

Anatoly

Anatoly and his mother also hid as the Aktion began, but the woman who sheltered them during the winter and the others in her house were taken away and killed.

Once again, Anatoly and his mother found themselves homeless on the streets and trying to avoid the soldiers and Polizei. After a few months, his mother, Serafima, was too weak from malnourishment and too ill to continue hiding. She was shot on July 28, four days after Anatoly's thirteenth birthday, leaving the teen alone. He continued to live on the streets, hunting for food in the trash and avoiding the soldiers. However, as the effects of starvation and illness weakened him, surviving became more difficult. Less than a month after his mother's murder, he got hit by a car and ended up in the hospital with a broken leg. Remaining in the ghetto was becoming more of a death sentence, and getting hit by the car enabled Anatoly to be taken away from the horror and placed in the hospital. It probably saved his life.

Lova

Realizing the situation they were in, others began looking for ways to escape the ghetto. Sometime before the Purim Aktion, eleven-year-old Lova Kravetz's father, Abram, made plans to escape and join the partisans. He begged his wife, Lisa, to let him take Lova with him. The Kravetz family tried to escape Minsk when the war began, and their house had been bombed. That time, Lisa had taken the children and fled to the nearby town of Lagoysk, where her relatives lived. As they walked toward Lagoysk at night, the flames from Minsk lit up the countryside and made it possible to see. However, when they had reached Lagoysk, the German army had already arrived, so they turned back to Minsk, where Abram found them again. Now, Lisa refused to let Abram take Lova on his escape attempt from the ghetto. Abram embraced his son and promised that after he reached the partisans, he would return for the whole family.

Lova, his mother, and his siblings (Maya, Boris, and Hanna) remained in the ghetto and waited for his return. They never saw him again and assumed his attempt to reach the partisans must have failed.

When the Purim Aktion began, Lova and Maya crawled under the barbed wire that surrounded the ghetto and narrowly escaped. On that fateful day, while his mother worked, his older sister, Hanna, and younger brother, Boris, remained at home. After the Aktion, Lova and Maya crept back into the ghetto looking for their family. They found their mother who had returned from work but discovered Hanna and Boris had been killed. While dealing with their grief, they found shelter in another part of the ghetto, living in a house of strangers.

The brutality displayed during the Purim Aktion surpassed even the previous ones. The atrocities included targeting the orphanage within the ghetto. Of all the horrible events experienced in the ghetto, the murder of an estimated two hundred orphaned children demonstrated that no one received mercy. To the Jewish people living in the ghetto, it seemed that evil knew no bounds. The soldiers gathered the children, mercilessly threw them into a pit, and buried them alive. As this horrible murder took place, several Nazi officers appeared to observe the deaths of the shrieking children, including the general commissioner of Belarus, Wilhelm Kube.

Despite taking an active role in planning the murders of the Jews of Belarus, early in his career, Kube wrote to Himmler to protest the "sadistic" way that the SS massacred thousands of Jews and Belarusians in the town of Slutsk the previous October. He complained that "to bury seriously wounded people alive who worked their way out of their graves again is such a base and filthy act that the incidents...should be reported to the Führer (Hitler)."[8] However, it seems that Kube's conscience had undergone a transformation since that letter, as he stood silently alongside Adolf Eichmann,[9] the Nazi SS official responsible for overseeing much of the transportation of Jews to their deaths. The Israelis captured, tried, and hanged Eichmann for his crimes in 1962. During the trial, Eichmann attempted to portray himself as a low-level functionary who was only following orders.[10]

In a gesture so bizarrely terrible it is almost incomprehensible, Kube threw candy to the children as they stood in the hole that would become their grave. Whether he meant this act to be a sickening attempt to ease his conscience or an act of pure cruelty is impossible to say.

Kube's actions are an enigma. He made antisemitic statements, comparing Jewish people to viruses, and spoke of exterminating them like rats, yet when ordered to murder the Hamburg Jews, he hesitated because of their shared German culture and because he knew many were decorated veterans who fought for Germany in World War I. In the end, he deferred the responsibility for their murders to the Lithuanian Polizei collaborators under his command.

As a Lutheran minister, he also actively participated in the "German Christian Church" movement. This movement within German Christianity sought to combine Nazi ideology with elements of Christian teachings and create a version of German Christianity without Jewish influences. "German Christians" distorted the teachings of the Bible, replacing the historical Jewish Jesus portrayed in the writings of the New Testament with an "Aryan Jesus." It seems that the teachings of Jesus forbidding murder and commanding love for others did not prevent the man who once oversaw a church from ordering the murder of the Jewish men, women, and children placed under his authority. All too often history presents us with examples of people who commit great atrocities while proclaiming devotion to a faith, the tenets of which stand in opposition to the actions being carried out. The difficult question of how a civilized "Christian" nation such as Germany could carry out such atrocities is an important subject but is beyond the scope of this book.

Kube met his end about a year and a half after he presided over the liquidation of the Minsk ghetto orphanage. Yelena Mazanik, a member of the Belarussian underground, got a job as a maid in his house and killed him with a time bomb that she placed under his bed.

As the seemingly senseless brutality of the Aktionen continued, the Nazis searched for new ways to make mass murder more efficient. Although the killing squads of the Einsatzgruppen and the slow death by starvation, overwork, and Aktionen in the ghettos resulted in the death of tens of thousands of Jewish victims, the Nazis felt they could find better ways to continue their crimes.

In August 1941, Reichführer Heinrich Himmler, the commander of the SS, toured Minsk. He asked Einsatzgruppe B, which was operating in the area, to demonstrate their shooting method for disposing of Jews. One hundred Jewish people were brought from the prison in Minsk and shot in Himmler's presence. As Himmler examined the mass grave, the pressure of the dirt being piled onto the heap of bodies caused blood to squirt out of the ground and splatter on his uniform. Accounts claim Himmler almost fainted and was visibly shaken by the experience of watching the brutal murder of one hundred people. After speaking with the members of the Einsatzgruppe murder squad, Himmler expressed his concerns that having to shoot hundreds of men, women, and children at point-blank range could take a psychological toll on the soldiers, and a better method for killing Jews should be devised. Himmler's time in Minsk displayed the disconnect with the brutal reality of the Nazis carefully designed policies against the Jews. Far removed from the mass graves and ghettos, Hitler and the Nazi leaders often planned their wicked crimes but left it to their subordinates to perform the horrific murders.

After witnessing this event, Himmler sought a way to sterilize the murders to ease the weight of committing mass murder on his men's psyche. The search for a different method began.

It did not take long for the Nazis to come up with a new method of murder. In the early days of the Nazi regime, they designed a euthanasia program called Aktion T4 to "purify" German society of people with physical and mental disabilities. The German clergy protested the morally reprehensible action of this euthanasia program, resulting in its activities being shut down. The Nazis exported and repurposed their methods used in Aktion T4 to the east. This new horror appeared in Minsk in the spring of 1942.

Leonid

Leonid remembered the day well. He was sawing firewood for the German commandant when a gray van drove into the ghetto. The Nazis called a group of children playing nearby to come over and offered them candy. They told them to get their friends, and the soldiers would take them for a ride. Six or seven kids came over, and the soldiers lifted them into the back of the van. A soldier checked his watch as the van drove away. Soon they returned and opened the door, and Leonid saw the bodies of the children strewn across the floor of the van. He stood there in shock, having witnessed a test of the murderous *Gaswagen*. The Nazis constructed these customized vans with an airtight compartment into which the exhaust from the engine vented. This allowed the carbon monoxide produced by the engine to asphyxiate the helpless victims inside. It represents one of the first attempts by the Nazis to use gas rather than bullets to carry out mass murder. It removed the bloody violence of shooting people but prolonged the death and suffering of the victims. Unlike shooting, it could take as long as twenty minutes for the victims to succumb. Soon these vans became a common and terrifying sight in the ghetto. Their presence was yet another danger for the prisoners of the ghetto to fear once they learned of their purpose. They called them the *dushegubka*, Russian for "soul killer."

The Gaswagens played a key role in future Aktionen. Rather than gathering crowds of victims and loading them on trucks to be driven away to be shot, the Nazis could load them into the vans, drive outside the city to the mass graves, and unload the bodies.

Zoya

Zoya and her family avoided this fate through assistance from an unexpected quarter. Her father's carpentry skills impressed a Nazi officer who took a liking to him. He often told her father how he would be rich if he could live in Germany, because his craftsmanship would be in high demand. Knowing of another Aktion approaching, the officer warned her father to get his family out of the ghetto and bring them to the Gestapo headquarters. He promised to find work for them that would keep them safely out of the way during the Aktion. When they arrived, they were told they would be cleaning cars. They were led to a gray van. Inside the floor, an 8-inch tube protruded, covered with a wooden grate. Their task was to remove the grate and sweep out the floor. As they began, they found many small personal objects lodged in the grate including buttons, lighters, children's shoes, and handkerchiefs.

When they finished cleaning the van, it drove away, and another arrived. The process repeated as van after van appeared.

Zoya and her family worked there for three days, cleaning vans. They did not realize the function of these vans and only later understood that the Nazis were gassing and transporting hundreds of people from the ghetto to locations outside the city where the bodies were buried in mass graves or burned.

The increasing rate and scale of the Aktion that kept the Gaswagens running for three days was not an isolated incident. In 1942, the Nazis increased their speed and scale of the campaign of mass murder, and it would prove to be the deadliest year of the Holocaust. It has been estimated that "in mid-March 1942 some 75 to 80 percent of all victims of the Holocaust were still alive, while 20 to 25 percent had perished. A mere eleven months later, in mid-February 1943, the percentages were exactly the reverse."[11] The story of the Holocaust was about to enter its most horrific stage.

The previous stages of the Nazis' brutal attacks on Soviet Jews (including Belarusian Jews) had been overseen by a Nazi officer that Hitler referred to as "the man with the iron heart." SS Obergruppenführer Reinhard Heydrich played a key role in the Nazis' actions against the Jewish people from the beginning. He helped plan and implement Kristallnacht, the night when the Nazis violently attacked German Jews in 1938, burning synagogues and looting Jewish businesses. He later oversaw the Einsatzgruppen as the Nazis invaded the Soviet Union. He was a key figure in the discussions of the Final Solution at the Wannsee Conference, where in early 1942 the Nazis determined to wipe out the entire Jewish population of Europe. However, before he could oversee the new plan, a team of British-trained Czechoslovakian partisans assassinated him in Prague.

A few months after Heydrich's death, the Nazi high command began to implement the plans he designed. In nearby Poland, they began Aktion Reinhard, so named to honor the recently assassinated Heydrich. To facilitate this wave of murder, they began constructing extermination camps (commonly referred to as death camps).

Unlike concentration camps that functioned as holding facilities where people were used as slave labor while being starved to death (like the ghetto), death camps existed for a sole purpose: as efficient factories of death where large numbers of people could be erased from existence in minutes.

While the Einsatzgruppen had been murdering Soviet Jews since June 1941, Polish and Western European Jews had thus far largely escaped the degree of horror that their eastern brethren experienced. Under Operation Reinhard, they became the primary targets for annihilation. In 1942, the Nazis built four camps in Poland—Chelmno, Belzec, Sobibor, and Treblinka—designated as *Vernichtungslager* (extermination camps). Their single function was mass murder. When discussing death camps, an important historical clarification must be made. Auschwitz, although the most commonly known camp, was not built as a death camp. Initially, it functioned as a concentration camp, but the Nazis later constructed the Auschwitz-Birkenau site as a hybrid camp where more than a million people were murdered while many others were kept alive as slave labor. Both Auschwitz and Majdanek were concentration camps with a death camp function, yet they functioned as concentration camps for their entire existence. Death camps did not house workers with the exception of several hundred unfortunate souls selected as members of the *Sonderkommando* (Jewish prisoners forced to assist with the disposal of bodies). The victims who arrived in these camps spent less than an hour there before being murdered. The shocking reality of the efficiency of these death factories is demonstrated by the fact that a visitor touring one of the memorial sites today will spend longer in the death camp than those brought there to be murdered. The grim fact that very few from any of the death camps lived to tell about them attests to their horrible efficiency. Only seven prisoners survived Belzec, where between 450,000 and 600,000 people were murdered. At Treblinka, where nine hundred thousand (second only to Auschwitz) perished, only seventy people survived.

The death camp of Chelmno near Lodz was the first operational death camp. Here, the Nazis used Gaswagens as the primary means of murder. In Belzec, the second death camp the Nazis established in southern Poland on the border with Ukraine, the innovation of a stationary gas chamber appeared, operated by the exhaust of a tank engine.

Soon the pesticide Zyklon B replaced the carbon monoxide from engine exhaust, and some concentration camps such as Auschwitz-Birkenau were partly converted to a death camp function.

Under the plan that invented the death camps, the ghettos would be liquidated and the Jewish people from them sent by train to these camps to be killed. While Operation Reinhard primarily focused on Polish Jews, the Nazis in Belarus also increased their killing and built an extermination camp on the outskirts of Minsk.

Lova

In October 1942, Lova and Maya Kravetz waited for their mother to return from her job at the factory. One day, she did not return, and they heard that her entire work detail had been taken to Trostenets. They did not understand what this meant. Lova did not know that in the Nazis' efforts to liquidate the ghetto, they had established a place where ghetto residents could be murdered. The place they chose, a former collective farm on the outskirts of Minsk, would become the Maly Trostenets death camp. The Nazis loaded victims into a Gaswagen and drove them to Trostenets. By the time they arrived, everyone was dead, and the bodies were cremated. In addition to the Gaswagens, a train track led to the camp. Jewish victims from across Europe arrived by train in a small, forested location called Blagovshchina next to the camp. Here, more than thirty-two mass graves waited for victims who were to be shot and buried. Based on these graves alone, we can conclude a minimum of sixty thousand victims died here. Other estimates that include the presence of a crematorium inside the camp suggest that as many as half a million people perished on this site. Maly Trostenets was among the ten most deadly camps used in the Final Solution and the largest death camp on Soviet territory. The Nazis scattered the ashes of the victims on the farmland of Trostenets. When surveying this site, investigators found human ashes 1 meter (3 feet) deep in places.

The Nazis' efforts to burn their victims' bodies was the result of a discovery made by German troops in 1943. In the Katyn forest in Poland, German soldiers uncovered mass graves where the Soviets shot more than twenty thousand Polish military officers after occupying eastern Poland. The Nazis publicized this discovery as propaganda to demonstrate the Soviets' brutal nature. However, they realized that their crimes had the potential to be uncovered in a similar manner. They implemented Aktion 1005, a directive to burn murdered Jews' bodies to hide the evidence of their atrocities. Today, the mass graves and amount of human ash are a few signs of how many victims perished at Maly Trostenets.

Zoya

As the Nazis' efforts to murder the innocent Jews of Belarus increased, Zoya's family lost another member in late 1942. One day as her mother returned from work with a few boards for firewood, a guard grabbed the boards and pushed her out of the column. Zoya never saw her again. At this point, Zoya had lost half of her family including her grandparents, brother, and mother. Only her father and two sisters remained.

Sima

In July 1942, another pogrom took place. When Sima returned home from work on the night of July 28, she found that her mother and little sisters, Nechama and Berta, had been murdered. Thirteen-year-old Sima was devastated by this horrible loss. Scared and alone, she had no choice but to try to survive despite the overwhelming emotional trauma she had endured. One day, a Belarusian woman took pity on her and rescued her, hiding her for the remainder of the war. Sima was deeply grateful to find that someone cared for her and she was not an unwanted child.

Leonid

Leonid also lost more loved ones. He witnessed his father's brutal murder one day at the hands of a Nazi officer. In the ghetto, people were supposed to remove their hats when they saw a soldier. Leonid and his father were outside his grandmother's house when a Nazi commander walked up behind them and demanded to know why Leonid's father had not taken off his hat. His father turned around, saw the officer, and quickly removed his hat. He attempted to explain that he had not seen the officer since he was behind him. The officer snapped, "You didn't see us? Now you will see!" as he drew his pistol and fired. As they walked away, Leonid bent over the body of his father to catch his last words, "That is all."

Like the others, Leonid had no choice but to try to continue living. He still worked with the painting crew, but without his father's advice and camaraderie he felt very lonely and vulnerable.

Sometime after this, he lost his mother. She disappeared, and he heard she may have been taken to Maly Trostenets. Then his brother was captured during an Aktion. The soldiers had orders that the Aktion would last until 7:00 p.m. Leonid's brother and his friend hid and came out of hiding only after the shooting stopped. A German accompanied by two Polizei stopped them. The German told the Polizei that "Befehl ist Befehl" (orders are orders). The Aktion was officially over, so he instructed the Polizei to release the boys. After the German left, the Polizei reasoned that if they released the boys, they would have to hunt them down again. Overhearing this, both boys ran for their lives, but the Polizei opened fire, killing Leonid's brother. He was barely a teenager when his life was cruelly ended.

Seeing the rate of killing increasing and the population of the ghetto continuing to shrink, people realized their days were numbered if they stayed there, and many tried to escape.

While some escaped, the Nazis began shipping others away from Minsk. Leonid found himself taken from work, put on a train with about two thousand others from the ghetto, and shipped to the concentration camp of Majdanek near Lubin, Poland. There he received an assignment to a work detail and was moved from camp to camp, surviving Auschwitz and Dachau. However, almost all the other Jewish residents of Minsk on the train did not have the same luck and met their untimely end in Majdanek, a fact Leonid discovered only after the war.

Zoya

One day, Zoya overheard people planning to escape the ghetto and join local partisans.

One day in October 1943, she and a friend followed the men whose plan she overheard, slipped under the fence, and left the ghetto. They walked out of Minsk, following the men and knowing that if they were caught, they would be shot. Zoya hoped to find safety with the partisans and then return to the ghetto to help her father and sisters escape. Once she reached the partisan camp, she received heartbreaking news. The day after she had escaped the ghetto, it had been liquidated. Everyone who remained was murdered or shipped to concentration or death camps. Zoya realized her entire family had been killed and that if she had stayed another day, she also would not have survived.

The story of the Minsk Ghetto ends on October 21, 1943. One hundred thousand people, both local Belarusian Jews and German Hamburg Jews who suffered together in the cramped quarters behind barbed wire in this tortured city, were dead. Only a handful survived inside the ghetto until the end. One group remained in their malina, hiding underground for eight months until the Red Army arrived in July 1944. Half of them perished, but thirteen survived as the last residents of the ghetto of Minsk. Most of those who survived the ghetto did so only by leaving it with the help of those on the outside who hid them or by joining the partisans. Our story now turns to these experiences.

CHAPTER 4

Fighting Back:
The Partisans

———— ∞ ————

The 2008 film *Defiance* became one of the first attempts to tell a wartime story of the Belarusian Jews on screen by following the experiences of the Bielski partisan unit. The Bielski group was one of two Jewish partisan units operating in Belarusian territory during the war, and their story is one of amazing survival and bravery. The Jewish director of the film, Ed Zwick, explained how he grew up with a concept of the passive Jewish victims during the Holocaust who went like sheep to the slaughter.[12] In fact, many Jewish people resisted. For example, even when all hope was lost, prisoners blew up a crematorium in Auschwitz, attempting to slow the killing process. It is a common misconception that if the Jews had fought back, somehow the Holocaust could have been prevented. Many of the survivors express their desire that this deeply offensive and inaccurate misconception be corrected. Zwick's *Defiance* is a great example of the overlooked story of Jewish heroism. It depicts how small bands of Jewish resistance fought to survive and defend their loved ones even as the Nazis crushed entire armies across Europe.

In one particularly powerful scene in the film, Tuvia Bielski, the leader of the group, welcomes new members who escaped the ghettos. He tells them, "This is the only place in all of Belarus where a Jew can be free." Life among the partisans in the forest offered not only freedom but the best chance of survival.

Resistance groups opposed the Nazi occupation across Europe and often assisted Jewish people in their escape. However, Belarus proved to be an ideal location for partisan resistance.

The following factors helped shape the partisan movement in Belarus. Due to the quick collapse of the Soviet front lines during the initial weeks of the war, large numbers of soldiers found themselves unable to escape. Knowing they would not be treated well as prisoners of war (POWs), many hid in the forest and formed partisan units. Many local people, suffering at the hands of the Nazis and hoping to drive the invaders from their land, joined these soldiers.

Realizing that they could not hold their ground, Soviet forces began supporting and developing partisan activity. Belarus lay strategically on the road to Moscow, and the German supply lines for their advancing armies ran right through the region. Furthermore, the rural countryside, covered in thick forests with only small villages scattered throughout, was ideal for partisan activity. The partisan movement in Belarus soon succeeded in establishing large "partisan zones" (areas under de facto partisan control). The Nazis avoided these areas at night and dared enter only with a strong force of soldiers.

The Soviets attempted to supply the partisans by air, but as the German army groups advanced, a gap opened between the northern and central German armies. The Soviets exploited this break in the front line near the Belarusian city of Vitebsk, naming it the Vitebsk gate. Weapons, orders, and other vital supplies and information flowed from Moscow, between the two Nazi armies, and directly to partisan units in Belarus. Despite this, supplies remained limited, and people often made do with homemade weapons.

To meet their needs, the partisans developed weapons manufacturing and repair shops as well as propaganda printing presses, forest schools (where children could be educated and disciplined), and radio units that attempted to maintain contact with Moscow.

While many Jewish people fought with the Soviet partisan groups, many others could not. Due to the supply challenges, partisan groups usually required that potential recruits supply their own weapons. Since they were fighting a war and living in rough conditions in the forest, the partisans wanted only people who were physically fit and able to fight. They would not allow families with children, elderly, or ill people to join them, since this would weaken the unit. Additionally, some partisans were antisemitic and did not trust Jews.

In response to these circumstances, two Jewish partisan groups developed in Belarus. They focused on protecting survivors rather than seeking ways to attack the Nazis or collaborators. While the Bielskis operated in western Belarus, a second unit led by Simcha Zorin operated closer to Minsk. About eight hundred people survived in the Zorin unit, many of whom were survivors of the Minsk Ghetto. Bielski and Zorin's "family camps" were the largest and most successful examples of Jewish partisans giving shelter to their fellow Jews, although a similar phenomenon took place on a much smaller scale in the Parczew Forest in Poland. [13]

In other places in Europe, such as the Warsaw Ghetto in Poland, the Jewish underground staged armed resistance to stop deportations to the death camps. Although they diverted large numbers of Nazi troops, such resistance ended with a heroic last stand. The Warsaw partisans were crushed by tanks and aircraft and forced from their bunkers to be shot or shipped to a death camp.

In the Minsk Ghetto, the underground used a different approach: discreet actions as opposed to direct confrontation. Despite the danger, they smuggled many people out of the ghetto while others like Zoya escaped on their own to find one of the partisan groups operating in the area. The Judenrat assisted in this process by carefully removing names from the lists they kept for the administration of the ghetto, thus making people administratively disappear from the Nazis. Often the partisans requested that the Judenrat and underground in the ghetto send them people with particular skill sets including medical professionals or those who could work on weapons. Even children and teens had a role in the resistance. They often functioned as guides, leading groups escaping the ghetto to safety deep in the forest. The presence of these partisan groups in the nearby forest, combined with other facts such as the Minsk Ghetto being surrounded by barbed wire (which was easy to cut through or slip under) gave the underground the option of escape rather than fighting as their fellow Jews in Warsaw had done.

The remainder of this chapter will discuss three types of partisan experiences: escaped POWs who joined the partisans, Jewish civilians who joined Soviet partisan units, and those who escaped ghettos and camps and joined the exclusively Jewish partisan units.

Lev

Lev, having left his family and plans for his future behind him to defend his country, began the war with the People's Militia. However, he did not serve with this unit for long. After spending a few months digging trenches on the Belarusian-Russian border, the German attack came. By October 1941, the advancing German army smashed into Lev's unit. The untrained militia was overwhelmed by the onslaught of artillery, tanks, and aircraft. Lev saw many of his comrades die, and those who survived were quickly captured. The Germans marched Lev and his fellow POWs to Smolensk, a Russian city near the Belarusian border, where thousands of prisoners were gathered in the square. A German officer barked orders in broken Russian, separating the POWs into groups. "Russians here, Ukrainians here," he shouted at the mass of prisoners. As the prisoners moved toward their designated areas, Lev heard the officer shout, "Jews over here."

He began to head toward the group of Jewish prisoners, but something made him stop. He realized that he should not admit to being Jewish. He longed to be with his people, but held back and instead joined the Russian prisoners, giving a false Russian name. After separating all the prisoners, the Nazis killed the Jewish soldiers. Lev's premonition had saved his life. Lev and the Russian prisoners marched to the train station to be sent to Baranavichy in western Belarus where the Nazis had established a POW camp. In the camp, they received soup made from rotten potatoes and 150–200 grams of bread a day (about 7 oz.). Although this was not enough food to live on, they were fed more than those living in the Minsk ghetto. Despite getting a little more food, being a POW was still dangerous.

The conditions in the camp were filthy, and prisoners began to die of typhus, dysentery, and other ailments. Around twenty prisoners died every day. The horrible conditions were typical of the Nazi treatment of Soviet

POWs. They treated Soviets much worse than those of other nationalities, such as Americans or British, since they felt Slavs were racially inferior to Anglo-Saxons. It is estimated that as many as three million Soviet POWs died at the Nazis' hands during the war. The Nazis created the "hunger plan" to deliberately starve the Soviets, motivated by their theories that Slavs were inferior and a desire to depopulate the Soviet Union to make room for German settlers.

If the horrible circumstances of being a Soviet POW were not bad enough, Lev also had to worry that his Jewish identity would be discovered. A Nazi officer, Sonderführer Müller, worked in the camp. Müller constantly attempted to identify Jews or Communists among the prisoners so they could be separated and killed.

After a few weeks in the camp, Lev was so weak that he felt that he would die soon. He heard that the Germans wanted workers to help pick potatoes outside the camp. He went to the fence and spoke to one of the guards in German. He introduced himself (using his fake Russian name, Piotr Gusev) and told the guard he had been a student in Moscow and would like to work. His German impressed the guard, who released him to work in the fields. This provided him the chance to get potatoes as well as food that the local peasants smuggled to the prisoners under carts of hay.

Although the potatoes saved Lev from starving, he contracted typhus due to the unsanitary conditions in the camp and ended up in the barracks for sick soldiers. One day, Sonderführer Müller appeared to inspect the barrack. The guard told him that Lev had been a student in Moscow and could speak a little German. "But is he a Jew?" Müller demanded. "Nein," the guard replied, certain that Lev was not Jewish. You can imagine the fear Lev felt as he heard this conversation and the relief he experienced when Müller seemed satisfied and left the barracks.

Being a courageous young man, Lev wished to die on the battlefield. The thought of dying in the prison camp depressed him. His thoughts often turned to escape. When spring came and his health returned, he decided he was going to take a daring risk and escape or die trying.

On May 10, 1942, a bright, sunny day, Lev and the rest of the work detail marched out through the gate. On the road heading to their worksite, Lev asked the guard who often treated him kindly if he could step off the road to relieve himself. Once he reached the forest, he waited until the column moved down the road, and then he ran for his life. He heard shots behind him but did not stop. He did not intend to be captured again and was carrying a razor that he planned to use to take his own life to prevent being returned to the POW camp.

He ran out of the forest and found himself on the edge of a lake. He spotted two men fishing and asked where he could find partisans. One pointed in the direction he should go and said, "If you are searching, you will find them." After walking through the woods for hours, he heard a rooster crow and headed toward the sound. He found a small cottage where a woman and her teenage son lived. They provided him with dry clothing and food and hid him in the barn. Later, the woman explained that Germans and Polizei often came to her house. She asked him to go and hide in the forest until the partisan comrades came to get supplies from her.

That evening, the Soviet partisans showed up, and Lev hurried out to meet them. They took him deeper into the forest and introduced him to their commander, Captain Fedotov. Lev told the captain his real name (the first time he used it since inventing a Russian name) and shared his story.

He was assigned to help in the kitchen while he adapted to the partisan lifestyle. After the partisans began to trust him, they gave him a weapon. He became a scout and then the commander of military intelligence for the unit. He learned to ride a horse and often rode through the countryside, gathering information.

His partisan unit fought in the Hantsavichy district of the Pinsk region in southern Belarus. They later joined the Pinsk partisans led by Vasily Zakharovich Korzh, a man who received the title "Hero of the Soviet Union" for his actions.

After over two years of fighting with the partisans, Lev's war ended when his unit met up with advancing Red Army troops on July 7, 1944, in the outskirts of Pinsk. For his war service, Lev received the Order of the Red Star, the Order of the Great Patriotic War in the First Degree, a Partisan of the Great Patriotic War, and other medals. While Lev had been a soldier before joining the partisans, many civilians and even children also became partisans.

Lova after the war

Lova

After losing his mother, Lova began sneaking out of the ghetto to find food or a way to escape. Hearing of the partisans and after several narrow escapes in Minsk, Lova set out to find them. He joined a partisan unit and received the task of being a forest guide. This meant returning to the ghetto to lead others out. Lova risked his life twice by sneaking back into the ghetto. The first time he went back for his only surviving relative, his younger sister Maya. The partisans needed skilled individuals and gave him instructions regarding who to bring out. When friends and family of these people heard of a chance to get out, Lova found himself with more than thirty others wanting to escape. Leading such a large group over 40 km would be dangerous, but Lova made a plan to get them all out. They joined a work detail that was on its way to the railroad station and then slipped away. After escaping the ghetto, he divided his party into smaller groups to prevent everyone from being killed or captured if they encountered soldiers. This tactic saved some lives, because as one group passed a factory, someone began shooting at them. They all ran for cover in the forest, but several people were killed. They faced other dangers on the journey with several people drowning in the swamps and rivers. However, Lova successfully led the majority of his group through these dangers to the partisans.

At first, Lova served with the Parkhomenko partisan unit created by Zorin and a Russian POW named Ganzenko. This unit was a fighting group, but as more Jews fled the ghetto, Zorin created his own unit to protect Jewish survivors. Knowing that his sister would only be accepted in the Zorin group, Lova left Parkhomenko, and like many other ghetto survivors, he joined Zorin's unit.

Mikhail

For fifteen-year-old Mikhail Treister, the partisans would prove to be his only hope. Imprisoned in the Minsk Ghetto, he lied about being a shoemaker in order to get work. After several years working in German factories, he and his coworkers were taken to a prison camp set up on Shirokaya Street. Those who were unfortunate enough to be in this camp were destined to be taken to the Maly Trostenets death camp in a Gaswagen. As Mikhail awaited his fate, he recognized Naum Epstein, a ghetto official who arrived with a list of skilled workers that the Nazis needed. As he read the names off, the fortunate workers shouted out that they were present and stepped forward. Mikhail knew that he did not have enough skill to be considered a valuable worker. Suddenly a name was read off: "Naum Rosin!" No one answered, and almost before he realized what he was doing, Mikhail yelled, "Here" and stepped out of formation. Epstein did not betray the fact that he knew Mikhail was not Rosin, and he was taken back to the ghetto with the other skilled workers. Using this false identity, Mikhail knew he had escaped the immediate danger of being taken to Maly Trostenets, but it was far too dangerous to remain in the ghetto. He slipped out of the ghetto and soon met partisans from the Ponomarenko group. After they learned he had escaped the ghetto and could repair shoes, they allowed him to stay with them. He hoped to do something heroic and could not stand repairing shoes in the partisan camp. Since his mother and sister were still in the ghetto, he asked for permission to serve as a guide to smuggle people out. Like Lova, he risked his life to sneak back into the ghetto to rescue others. He had a list of skilled people the partisans wanted to rescue, and soon he had a group of twenty-five to thirty people gathered. After leading them out of the ghetto at night, they stopped to rest when the sun rose. Some of the adults wanted to continue while Mikhail insisted they wait until dark. As they discussed what to do, a young shepherd saw them. They attempted to bribe him so he would not report them, but everyone was uneasy, so Mikhail agreed to move during daylight. They split into three groups and started out with Mikhail's group bringing up the rear. The first two groups were caught in an open area near a highway and were attacked by a group of Germans and local police. All of one group and half of the other were killed. Only Mikhail's group survived without casualties.

Memories of that day haunted Mikhail throughout his life as he wondered if he was responsible for these deaths and if it would have been better to have insisted they wait until night and risk being reported by the shepherd boy. Despite the tragic deaths of some of his party, his heroic actions saved his mother, sister, and a number of others from almost certain death in the ghetto.

After this dangerous mission, Mikhail built himself a rifle from old parts but was sent back to the partisan shoemaker shop he hated. One day, he refused to work, and the shoemaker tried to force him back to the shoemaking dugout at gunpoint. After this, Mikhail was finally able to convince the commander to let him be a fighter. Ultimately, like most Jewish partisans, he ended up with the Zorin group where he served for the remainder of the war.

Zoya

Zoya also headed for Zorin's group. After slipping out of the ghetto the day before it was destroyed, Zoya wandered through the forest and abandoned villages for days, since she did not have a guide like Lova or Mikhail. She and a friend spent several frightening nights in the forest as they searched for the partisans. They met several boys on horseback, wearing red ribbons attached to their clothes. However, these young partisans did not trust them and accused the girls of being sent by the Nazis to poison them. Frightened by this accusation, the girls ran away. Fortunately, after spending several more days lost in the forest and eating grass, they found a group of partisans who took them to the Zorin group. On the way to the partisan camp, Zoya became separated and was once again lost and alone in the forest.

That night, she was traumatized when she thought she heard a baby crying in the dark forest. Later, she found out that it had been an owl. Finally, once she reached the partisan camp, they gave her work in the kitchen as well as washing bandages and cutting firewood. Living in the forest with the partisans was hard. The winters were brutally cold, and to make things even more unpleasant, in the summer, the forest was filled with mosquitoes and swarms of wasps. The partisans gathered mushrooms and berries in the forest and food from the nearby villages. Many villagers gladly supported the partisans, but at times, partisan groups took food by force to survive. The partisans had several cows that provided milk to supplement their diet. They dug long trenches in the forest and lined them with tree trunks. The camp consisted of four long dugouts with hundreds of people living in each. Zoya remembers how painfully uncomfortable it was lying on these logs at night and using wood for her pillow.

The Zorin group, in addition to fighting the Nazis, focused on running a forest refuge and hospital. The members of the group who went to the villages to collect food often did so on horseback. While most other Belarusian partisan groups accepted only fighting-age people with their own weapons, these groups sent their wounded to the Zorin group. To bring a little normalcy to the forest life and to help with hygiene, the group constructed a *banya* (a traditional Slavic sauna).

The unit moved its camp several times, as the Nazis occasionally launched large search efforts, using troops with dogs and Rama scout planes overhead to locate the partisan camps. In 1944, as the Red Army began driving the Nazis out of Belarus, Zorin and a detachment of partisans battled a group of Nazis. A number of partisans died in this fight, and Zorin was shot in the knee. The severity of his wound meant that his leg needed to be amputated, and Zoya was one of the partisan nurses who helped care for him as he recovered.

After the liberation of Minsk in 1944, Zoya hitched a ride with some Red Army soldiers into the city. At fourteen years old, she now began to attempt to rebuild her life. She went to her grandparents' house but found it occupied by strangers. With no one to take her in, her only choice was to go to an orphanage.

Alexander

While Mikhail, Lova, and Zoya lived with Zorin's Jewish partisans, Alexander, who lost his family in the first days of the war, joined a non-Jewish Soviet partisan unit in eastern Belarus near Mogilev. Soon he was involved in fighting and gathering intelligence. However, since his unit did not have access to portable radio transmitters, the only way they could relay information was by traveling to meet intelligence officers from the Red Army on foot. This risky endeavor required crossing the front lines between the German and Russian armies through the Vitebesk gate. Alexander went on this mission in 1942 and again in 1944. On his first trip in October 1942, he and other partisans went all the way to Moscow. They did not return to the front lines until May 1943. His trip took seven months. By then, Alexander was nineteen years old, and the partisans appointed him the commander of the 600th partisan detachment's intelligence service.

That July, he led a group of partisans on a sabotage mission to blow up the water tower at the Mogilev-1 railroad station. He also helped defeat the Nazi garrisons in Belynichy and Paskovo and derailed a train as part of another sabotage mission.

During his service, Alexander was wounded twice. The first time, he was shot in the lung. He found himself lying in a forested swamp, bleeding profusely and thinking he would not live to be twenty years old. However, a military scout plane spotted him and sent someone to rescue him and take him to a military hospital. The doctors who treated him expressed surprise that he survived, saying that the amount of blood loss he experienced should have been fatal. However, he recovered and returned to the war, only to be wounded again the next year. This wound in his left arm made him unable to play his beloved violin.

After his second recovery, he continued to fight and took part in the liberation of his home city of Mogilev.

CHAPTER 5

For Whom the Bells Toll: The Fate of the Belarusian Village

∞

ven today, a visitor to Belarus will be struck by the dichotomy in the society. In the capital, you see a beautiful and modern European city, but driving an hour outside the city takes you into another world. Nestled in the thick forest, small villages still dot the landscape. The sight of a few small houses and gardens along a dirt road gives a glimpse into the isolated, rural life of many Belarusians. It feels like stepping back in time and disconnecting from the modern, fast-paced life of the cities. During the occupation, the Nazis did not have the manpower to maintain a presence in all the villages, so they sent patrols through the region, often leaving destruction in their wake. The Nazis carried out collective punishment of whole villages, targeting those suspected of hiding Jews or assisting partisans for the most brutal treatment. To this day, quiet clearings in the forest lie empty where families once lived, farming for their livelihood.

The village of Khatyn, about 50 km outside Minsk, was once such a village. Today, visitors find themselves in a quiet clearing in the forest. The places where homes once stood are marked by haunting reconstructions of each house's foundation and chimney. Walking through a re-creation of an open gate (a reminder of Belarusian hospitality), one finds the names and ages of the former residents inscribed on the chimney. The names are those of the approximately twenty-five families that called Khatyn home.

They lived in relative peace until March 22, 1943, when Nazi forces appeared. Earlier that day, a unit called Schutzmannschaft Battalion 118 (which consisted of Ukrainian nationalists who willingly fought alongside the Nazis) traveled through the area, and partisans ambushed them. The partisans killed the Nazi commander, Hauptmann (Captain) Hans Wöllke. Wöllke was a former Olympic shotput champion for Germany and a personal friend of Hitler. After this attack, the Ukrainians were joined by an SS unit, the Dirlewanger Brigade, consisting of German criminals who chose military service to avoid going to prison. Both units had reputations for their exceptional brutality. Some members of Schutzmannschaft 118 had assisted the Nazis at the Babi Yar massacre in Ukraine. Babi Yar was one of the largest massacres of the Einsatzgruppen, where the Nazis and Ukrainians murdered more than thirty-three thousand Jewish people from Kyiv in two days in the first of many massacres on that site. Their brutality would be demonstrated yet again to the villagers of Khatyn.

Assuming the villagers supported the partisans who had attacked them and determined to avenge Wölke's death, the units surrounded the village, dragged the sleeping residents from their beds, and forced them into a barn in the center of the village. They lit the barn on fire and machine-gunned anyone who escaped the flames. After murdering the villagers, they burned the village to the ground. Four children hid during the attack and survived, and one child and man survived inside the burning barn. A statue of the man, Joseph Kaminsky, greets those who visit Khatyn today. He stands erect, holding the limp body of his son who he tried in vain to rescue from the ashes of the barn.

Kaminsky, the "Unbowed Man" at Khatyn

German soldiers burning a village

Khatyn was not an isolated instance. The Nazi occupiers burned more than five thousand villages in Belarus, including many Jewish shtetls. In 628 of these villages, they murdered the inhabitants, leaving nothing but smoldering ruins and burned bodies behind them as they had done in Khatyn.

Today, Khatyn is the national war memorial of Belarus. In the "Graveyard of Villages," one can find a collection of boxes inscribed with the names of 186 villages that were never rebuilt after the Nazis burned them and murdered the inhabitants. Each box holds soil taken from the sites where the villages once stood. A bell rings every thirty seconds, filling the site with a powerful reminder, as it is estimated that one Belarusian perished every thirty seconds during the war. It is believed that as many as 25 percent of Belarusian citizens perished during the Nazi occupation. Although the Nazis primarily targeted Jewish people, their killing machine also inflicted horrible damage on the Slavic Belarusian population.

The fear of such brutal retaliation for hiding fleeing Jews occupied the minds of Belarusians who could help the desperate people. Despite the risk, a notable number of Belarusians risked their lives to protect their Jewish neighbors.

Yaakov

After traveling across Belarus from his father's frontline army post on the western border, Yaakov, his mother, and his brother Misha found their relatives' apartment empty, and they soon ended up in the Babruysk Ghetto. Yaakov witnessed horrors similar to what took place in the Minsk Ghetto. He watched as the Polizei raided his neighbors' apartment, murdered the six occupants, and stole their belongings. After carrying out these crimes, they forced other prisoners in the ghetto to dig a grave in the front yard and bury the unfortunate victims.

Yaakov's mother begged the rabbi who was on the Judenrat for work to feed her sons. After seeing the small boys and their desperate mother, he gave her a pass to work as a seamstress. One day, some soldiers who had served with Yaakov's father found her and explained that her husband died when their radio station got hit by a bomb during the initial attack. After delivering the sad news, they noticed the yellow patch she was wearing and realized that she was a prisoner in the ghetto. They warned her to escape the ghetto if she wanted any chance of survival.

The next day, these soldiers brought a pass for Yaakov, his mother, and her friend that allowed them to go outside the ghetto. His little brother crawled under the fence, and then the family could escape together. They met a kindhearted farmer on the road who offered the children a ride on his cart, and after finding out they were Jewish and had escaped from the ghetto, he let them hide in his banya.

They heard that everyone in the Babruysk Ghetto had been murdered when it was liquidated two weeks after their escape. The farmer became afraid after seeing signs warning that anyone who assisted Jews would be shot along with their entire family. He told them that they needed to leave, as he would not risk his family. Yaakov and his family wandered from village to village, hoping to find someone willing to help them despite the risk. At this point, they parted ways with the friends they had been traveling with since the war began. Since their friends did not look Jewish, they thought they could pretend to be Russian and remained in the village, staying in the school. Sadly, they were mistaken. When the Nazis arrived, they were suspicious of people staying in the school. One soldier took the young girl away, gave her some candy, and asked what her grandparents' names were. After hearing Jewish names, he drew his pistol and killed them.

As Yaakov, Misha, and their mother wandered, they created new identities to hide that they were Jewish. While they lived on the military base in Grodno before the war, they got to know an Armenian family whose father served with Yaakov's father. He often told them stories about life in Armenia. Yaakov's mother began using the stories her husband's comrade told to create a fictional Armenian husband with whom she lost contact due to the war. This story also explained why Yaakov did not look Slavic, suggesting his father was Armenian. The story had just enough facts and details about Armenia that they could tell it confidently.

In a small village called Pavlovichi, a woman who heard their story began to ask questions about their missing Armenian father. After some time, she excitedly informed the family that a man who matched their description lived nearby. To maintain her cover, Yaakov's mother begged to be taken to see the man who could potentially be her "husband." She insisted that she could not spend another night without him, so the villager took her to meet him. Of course, he was not her husband, but the villagers took pity on the family and allowed them to stay. The village elder introduced them to a woman whose husband was also serving in the army. The woman, Irina Masyukevich, invited the three refugees to live with her and her three children on their small farm with a horse, cow, and some poultry. Since Yaakov's mother was a graduate of a veterinary college, she was able to help Irina with her livestock.

The village elder knew they were Jewish, since it turned out his brother was the farmer who sheltered them right after they escaped from the ghetto. Concerned for their safety, he ordered them to dig a hole in Irina's barn to hide when the Nazis came to the village. Most of the time, village life was safe, but there were occasional close calls when the Nazis suddenly appeared.

Yaakov's first close call happened while he helped the local boys shepherding flocks of geese from the village. Some German soldiers passed by on motorcycles. Seeing the boys with about forty geese, they stopped and began shooting at the geese with their machine guns. They gathered the geese they had shot and drove away.

After the soldiers killed the geese, Yaakov and his brother went around to the nearby villages to beg for food. Several times the police stopped them and forced them to remove their pants so they could see if they had been circumcised. If Yaakov's father had not refused to allow his grandparents to circumcise him, they would have been caught. Even after the war, many Jewish people in the Soviet Union struggled with maintaining this traditional Jewish practice and potentially endangering their children by forever marking them as Jewish.

In the summer of 1943, their cover story claiming to be the family of an Armenian officer in the Red Army led to another dangerous situation. A unit of the Armenische Legion (Armenians who joined the Nazi army) came to the village. Armenia was part of the Soviet Union, which is why Yaakov's father served with an Armenian in the Red Army. However, many nations in the Soviet Union had nationalist movements that wished independence from the Russian-dominated Soviet Union. Ukraine, Lithuania, Armenia, and even Belarus had such groups, and many of them viewed the Nazis as liberators. The Nazis, in turn, gladly exploited any nationalist movements and actively recruited supporters of the movements into their ranks.

Yaakov's close call came when he and Misha encountered Nazi Armenians as they were begging for food. One soldier grabbed Yaakov and examined his hair. After doing so, he said that Yaakov was not Armenian. Another soldier intervened and explained that his mother was Russian so he was only half Armenian, which would explain the lack of Armenian physical traits. If it had not been for this second solider, his cover story may have been destroyed.

Before the men left, they brought a cartload of food and explained it was for the "Armenian children." Yaakov's mother told them if they had stolen the food from other people, she could not accept it, because the villagers would murder her family in revenge. The soldiers angrily left, leaving Yaakov and Misha confused as to why their mother rejected food when they were so hungry.

Another time, the Nazis came with a doctor and took all the children over the age of eight into a barn to examine them. Examining Yaakov, the doctor did not like the sound of his lungs and asked him his age. Yaakov said he was eight, and the doctor insisted that he should say six. Because of this lie, the Nazis did not select him for what would prove to be a horrible fate. They took twenty other children away and drained their blood to give transfusions to wounded German soldiers.

As the war progressed, Yaakov's mother began caring for sick and wounded partisans who stayed in Irina's barn. One day, a soldier came into the barn looking for eggs. Irina feared he would find the two partisans staying there and kill everyone on the farm. However, the partisans heard the soldier climbing into the loft and buried themselves in the hay. To everyone's' relief, the solider soon found enough eggs to satisfy him and left the barn without searching it carefully.

Despite these close calls, Yaakov and his family remained with Irina until the end of the war, living in constant uncertainty and fear.

Raisa

The Naimark family also sought refuge in the countryside. Samuel and Lubov Naimark lived in Mogilev in eastern Belarus with their daughter, Raisa. The family tragically lost their four-year-old son due to illness before the war. Samuel was a well-to-do shopkeeper. Estimates suggest that Mogilev's population was up to 50 percent Jewish. Due to its location near the eastern border with Russia, many Jewish residents had time to flee before the Nazis arrived.

When the war began, the bombing destroyed the Naimark's house, yet they remained in the city. A few months after the invasion, on September 25, the Nazis established a ghetto in Mogilev near the Dubrovenka Bridge. Eight-year-old Raisa watched as barbed wire surrounded their neighborhood. Because her mother did not look Jewish, she could remove her yellow patch and sneak out of the ghetto to find food. Since this ghetto had been established later than the one in Minsk, the Nazis began killing people within a few months of establishing it. They began shipping people to Auschwitz, and Samuel was among those who were sent to their deaths.

The Nazis also began taking many Jewish people out of the ghetto to the abandoned Dimitrov factory where they selected some as laborers and murdered the rest. They took a pregnant Lubov, Raisa, and her grandmother to the factory.

Lubov approached one of the guards with a daring plan. She told the guard they had made a terrible mistake. She said that her husband was Jewish, but she was not. The soldier believed her and released her and Raisa. They hurried home, only to be arrested and sent back to the factory. There Raisa spotted a room full of clothes and her grandmother's things among them. Realizing her grandmother had been killed, she snatched a bottle of French perfume from her mother and bravely ran to one of the guards, shouting that she did not want to die. Her mother followed and, with the perfume and some earrings, bribed the guard to release them.

After twice escaping the Nazis' hands, they fled into the forest where despite being ill with typhus, Lubov gave birth to a healthy baby girl whom she named Vera. They traveled to a village where they had relatives (the Gusarevichy family). They obtained false documents, and Lubov decided to join the partisans. She left Raisa with her aunt in the village and took Vera to join a partisan detachment. She promised to supply the aunt with food in exchange for taking care of Raisa.

Lubov often used Vera to avert suspicion, as nursing mothers were not usually part of partisan groups. At one point, she was arrested, beaten, and threatened that her baby would be shot in front of her if she did not divulge the information that her interrogators wanted. However, she and Vera survived all of this. She continued to nurse Vera for two years since she did not have enough food for her. The first time the baby spoke was to beg for food, and her first word was "give." One of Vera's earliest memories is being dropped in the snow by her desperate, exhausted mother who put her on a doorstep, planning to leave her and hoping that the people in the house would care for her. However, hearing her daughter's cries was too much for her, and she returned and picked her up.

Another time, the partisan unit was hiding in the woods as German soldiers passed by. Vera began to cough, and the commander made her mother lay on top of her to stifle the sound. Thankfully, Vera did not suffocate. Meanwhile in the village, Raisa's aunt was afraid the Nazis would come, so she told Raisa that she could sleep in the barn at night but had to leave during the day. Raisa resorted to searching the fields for frozen vegetables in order to survive. One day, while she occupied herself looking for food, the Nazis came to the village and burned it to the ground. Her aunt's refusal to allow her to stay with her was the only thing that saved her. Soon after this, the Russians began advancing through the region as they drove the Nazis back.

Raisa met a Russian soldier advancing with his unit who brought her to Mogilev. She begged on the streets until her mother and sister found her!

CHAPTER 6

Saving Countless Worlds: The Righteous Among the Nations

Whoever saves a life of Israel, it is considered as if he saved an entire world.

—Mishnah Sanhedrin 4:5

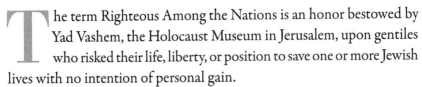

The term Righteous Among the Nations is an honor bestowed by Yad Vashem, the Holocaust Museum in Jerusalem, upon gentiles who risked their life, liberty, or position to save one or more Jewish lives with no intention of personal gain.

The stories of some of these people have been made famous by books or films. Steven Spielberg's masterpiece depicting the horrors of the Holocaust, *Schindler's List*, tells the story of Oskar Schindler, a German businessman who prevented hundreds of his Jewish employees from being deported to the death camps. The 2017 film *The Zookeeper's Wife* tells the story of Jan and Antonina Zabinski, a Polish couple who ran the Warsaw zoo and used it as a refuge for Jews escaping the ghetto. In her book *The Hiding Place*, Corrie ten Boom tells the story of how her family of Dutch watchmakers hid Jewish people. Another Dutch couple, Miep and Jan Gies, are immortalized in *The Diary of Anne Frank,* while various books and movies tell the story of the heroic efforts of diplomats like Raoul Wallenberg and Carl Lutz in Budapest, Hungary.

These famous stories represent only ten individuals from diverse backgrounds who did what they could to save the lives of many Jewish people. However, the stories of most of the more than twenty-seven thousand individuals recognized by Yad Vashem are not as well known. If it were possible, every one of these brave people and the things they did should be as well-known as the examples listed here.

The Nobel Prize-winning author and survivor of Auschwitz and Buchenwald, Elie Wiesel, reflected on the special nature of the Righteous Among the Nations: "Only a few had the courage to care. These few men and women were vulnerable, afraid, helpless. What made them different from their fellow citizens? Why were there so few?" The fact that twenty-seven thousand recognized Righteous Among the Nations represented a mere five thousands of one percent (.005%) of the estimated population of Europe at that time makes his question "why were there so few" even more poignant.

There is no clear answer to his question, as there are no apparent commonalities among the Righteous beyond their actions to save Jewish lives. They were men and women from across Europe and as far off as the United States, China, and Japan. There were Christians of every sect: Protestant, Orthodox, and Catholic, while others were Muslims, atheists, or Communists. They cannot be defined by race, nationality, religion, or political identity, only by their courage and humanity.

This chapter tells the stories of individuals whose names have been enshrined as Righteous Among the Nations for the role that they played in the lives of the Belarusian survivors whose stories are told within this book.

Their stories exude great courage and moral clarity. Finding their fellow humans in mortal danger, they risked their lives to give others a chance to live. Without their efforts and sacrifices, many of the people whose stories are told in this book would have joined the millions whose voices were silenced by the Nazis.

In Minsk, a group of such people found themselves witnessing the horrors that the Jewish people faced under the Nazis. They came from diverse backgrounds: a pastor, a professor, a kindergarten teacher, and a German Wehrmacht officer. Meeting at this critical hour, each had a unique role and position that enabled them to provide relief and deliverance to Jewish children.

Pastor Anton Ketsko

The hardships Anton Ketsko faced in life did not begin with the war. Born in the small Belarusian village Zamogilye (Rassvet, Minsk District), he was a devout Baptist. The Soviet government arrested him at the age of twenty-three for leading Bible studies in his village. In the USSR, the Communist regime's opposition to religion (described by Karl Marx as "the opium of the people") led to great efforts to suppress religious practice, including Bible teaching. They often arrested religious leaders, who could face beatings or execution for continuing their religious activity.

After his release from prison, Ketsko married Nina, and they moved to Minsk to raise their three children. In Minsk, he worked as a foreman for military building projects while secretly connecting with Baptist Christians whose churches had been closed as part of the Soviet crackdown on religion. They appointed him a presbyter so he could help minister in a large network of underground Christian meetings.

When the Nazis arrived in Belarus, Ketsko knew that they were not radical atheists like the Soviets, so he approached the new Nazi administration and asked for approval to begin conducting church meetings publicly. The Nazi official was suspicious and demanded to know how Ketsko could prove he was a Christian religious leader. Ketsko showed the officer papers that detailed his prison record under the Soviets for his faith as well as their refusal to allow him to serve in the Red Army, since they considered him a spreader of religious propaganda. The officer granted him approval to begin functioning as a Baptist pastor and gave him an old salt warehouse in the Nemiga neighborhood (close to the ghetto) to use as a church building.

While the Nazis allowed Ketsko to open a church, they also closed many of the state institutions that existed under the Soviets. This included the Maxsim Tank Belarusian State Pedagogical University where Vasili Orlov worked as a geography teacher after completing his PhD and his service in the Red Army. Out of work, Orlov soon got a job as a member of the city committee in charge of overseeing the abandoned children in the city's orphanages, a position that he would use to do as much good as possible.

With the Soviet government gone, the responsibility of administering the orphanages fell to the churches. The orphanage administration informed Ketsko that the Orthodox and Catholic churches agreed to take responsibility for two orphanages each and asked the new Baptist church to do the same. This meant being responsible for the food, clothing, and shelter for as many children as the city committee sent to him. Ketsko agreed, and soon Orphanages Numbers 2 and 7, and 126 children, became his responsibility. The church began fundraising and collecting donations to feed this large group of children. Ketsko traveled throughout Belarus, speaking at churches and raising money for the orphans of Minsk. A member of the Baptist church named Yakov Rapetzkii got involved and visited the orphanages to teach the children to pray and sing.

As the underground witnessed the increasing violence in the Minsk Ghetto and began to realize the extent of the Nazis' plan, they hurried to save Jewish children. Many were smuggled out of the ghetto and placed in orphanages. This was no easy task as many looked Jewish, their identification papers stated Jewish as their nationality, and they often spoke Russian with a Yiddish accent. Orlov began using his position in the city hall to issue false papers, changing names and nationalities, thus transforming Jewish children into Belarusians, Russians, or Poles. Some of these children were so young that they did not remember their true names and identities, knowing only the false identity crafted to protect them.

Irina

Many families made similar efforts to protect their children or younger relatives, sometimes making arrangements with the orphanage staff. Others lied on the forms that they filled out, listing false names and nationalities. Irina and her siblings were among these children. A friend of Irina's mother, a woman named Anna Shipro, worked with the underground. She snuck into the ghetto and took Irina and her brother and sister out in a cart under a heavy load, one by one. After months of breathing the stench of the ghetto air, Irina remembers almost being suffocated during the escape, yet soon she was outside the ghetto and could finally breathe fresh air without the lingering stench of death. To convince them to go with her, Anna lied and told them their mother was still alive and had sent her for them. Anna lived near Orphanage Number 2. She took the children there and enrolled them under false Russian names. After the war, Irina learned that the Nazis arrested and hung the heroic Anna for her work in the underground.

The Nazis systematically searched the orphanages for Jewish children and often brought in "racial experts" to evaluate whether the children were Jewish based on their physical features. Some orphanage staff turned over any Jewish children placed in their trust. Orlov began sending more Jewish children to Orphanages Number 2 and 7, knowing Ketsko and the staff would not betray them to the Nazis.

Orlov and Ketsko's efforts relied on the directors of the orphanages, Mariya Voronich of Number 2 and Vera Sparning of Number 7, to prevent the Nazis from finding the Jewish children placed under their care.

Like Orlov, Vera Sparning lost her job when the war began. Originally from Latvia, she worked at a kindergarten in a sanatorium for children suffering from tuberculosis. After it closed, she began helping the many orphaned children wandering the streets and then took the role of director at Orphanage Number 7. To protect the children under her care, she hung signs around the orphanage, warning of an outbreak of typhoid. She knew the fear of infectious disease would keep the Nazis away for a while.

As this network developed between Orlov, Sparning, Ketsko, and others, Ketsko continued to conduct church services. One day, a tall German officer entered the church for the service. He introduced himself to Ketsko as Gerhard Krüger. He explained that he was a Christian searching for a church to attend while he was stationed in Minsk as part of German military intelligence. Krüger found out about the Jewish children under Ketsko's care and demonstrated his willingness to help. He stole food from the Nazi supplies and created hidden pockets in his extremely long overcoat (he stood almost seven feet tall) and brought the supplies to Ketsko to feed the children.

Gerhard Krüger in his Wehrmacht army uniform (on left)

Krüger's role as an officer in the German army gave him access to the Nazi plans for Aktionen in Minsk, and he began passing information to Ketsko and his helper, Yakov Rapetzkii, warning them when a search of an orphanage was imminent. This allowed the staff to hide the children whose looks or accent appeared too Jewish. The orphanages constructed hiding places in the basement to conceal the Jewish children. Fearing the (nonexistent) typhoid that Sparning's signs warned about, the Nazis stayed outside and ordered the children brought out for examination. This made it easier to hide the Jewish children inside the orphanage.

However, they still faced a problem, because the orphanage records showed the number of children living there. They knew if the number did not match, the Nazis would be suspicious. Ketsko developed a risky solution to this problem. When Krüger warned of a raid, Vera Sparning and Mariya Voronich began hiding the Jewish children. Ketsko collected children from other members of his church and brought them to the orphanage along with his own daughters to take the place of the Jewish children. His eldest, Valentina, remembers being taken to the orphanage during a raid. Only being five years old, she was too young to comprehend what was happening and did not realize the danger her father subjected her to in order to protect the Jewish children under his care.

Anatoly

Through the efforts of this brave group of people, seventy-two Jewish children survived the war. Anatoly was among them. After recovering from being struck by a car in the ghetto, he was placed in Orphanage Number 7 under Sparning's care. He remembered being surprised when he first entered the orphanage and saw a large number of Jewish children. He recalled how Vera hid children in the cellar and how she set up a shoe repair shop to teach the older children a practical skill and make money for the orphanage.

Lydia

Lydia Petrova's parents died in the ghetto, leaving her orphaned at age three. Her first memories consist of wandering in the street, infested with lice and begging for food, surrounded by burning buildings, and watching Nazi soldiers march by. Finally, someone took her to Orphanage Number 2 on Krasivaya Street.

She remembered how children who did not look Jewish were baptized, labeled as Christians, and given crosses to wear by a priest who visited them and gave them bread. This was likely Yakov Rapetzkii from Kestsko's church. The children turned the cross necklaces he gave them into dolls and played with them. Lydia recalled that a large portrait of Hitler hung in the orphanage, and they sometimes gathered and sang in front of it. The orphanage staff shaved the children's heads to prevent lice. However, this served a secondary purpose of hiding the dark or curly hair that the Nazis looked for to detect Jewish children. Lydia recalls being rushed into a dark cellar to hide when the Nazis came searching for Jewish children.

Children from Orphanage Number 7
(arrow points to Lydia)

For Lydia and many of the children, the conditions in the orphanage were defined by always being afraid, hungry, and sick.

Irina

Irina was also sick after escaping the ghetto and being placed in the orphanage. The staff placed her in the isolation ward. When her older sister, Alla, tried to visit her to see how she was doing, the staff slapped her for violating the isolation.

Orlov, Krüger, Ketsko, Sparning, and Voronich worked behind the scenes to protect the children, but they could not shelter them from all the horrors of war.

Once an orphanage employee told the children that the war would not end until all the Jews were killed. You can imagine the scarring impact that could have on a child. One of the other Jewish girls in the orphanage feared the Nazis would return to kill her. Even after the war ended, she was unable to cope with the psychological damage this statement caused, refusing to believe the war was over because she was still alive. She could not imagine that the Nazis had failed.

Late in the war, bombing damaged Orphanage Number 2, and the children had to be placed somewhere else. The staff made efforts to find families who would take a child into their home. Lydia was so ill and infested with lice that they had a difficult time finding someone to care for her. Finally, a railway worker and his family took her in, and she stayed with them for the remainder of the war.

After the war, Sparning regained her job working with children suffering from tuberculosis. She married and adopted a girl from the orphanage. She passed away in 1984, and in 2001, Yad Vashem recognized her as a Righteous Among the Nations.

The Red Army's liberation of Minsk did not bring freedom to everyone. The returning Soviets arrested Orlov and Ketsko as collaborators and accused them of working with the Germans. The children they saved wrote letters on their behalf, expressing gratitude to the men who risked their own lives to save them. These letters eventually secured Orlov and Ketsko's release. One of the letters written on Orlov's behalf states the following:

> We are grateful to Comrade Orlov. Our hearts are overwhelmed with delight and our eyes clouded with tears of joy. The S.D. (Nazi Intelligence Service) is gone and there will be no more ghetto! Many

were afraid to acknowledge us, but there was one man who didn't turn his back on us. Comrade Orlov worked under the Germans overseeing the children institutions. He knew that he could suffer, but he did his best to save and hide children from the horror of the ghetto and hunger.

Ketsko served three years in a Soviet gulag before the children's appeal led Soviet forces to free him. In 2005, Orlov, Ketsko, and Voronich of Orphanage Number 2 were also recognized as Righteous Among the Nations.

Gerhard Krüger did not receive this honor for his role in supplying food or warning the orphanage staff of impending raids, although he risked his well-being to do so. However, in 2004, his son, Horst, visited Minsk and met Ketsko's daughters, who arranged for him to meet a group of the children who survived because of his father's efforts. Among this group was Lova Kravetz who, although he had not been in the orphanages, encountered Krüger directly during his efforts to escape the ghetto.

Lova

After his mother's murder at Trostenets, Lova attempted to find food for himself and his sister. After many close calls with the police and soldiers, he made up his mind that he would escape, try to find the partisans, and come back to bring her to safety. As he slipped out of the ghetto, it seemed that his luck had run out. Two Belarusian Polizei stopped him, saw his curly hair, and realized that he was Jewish. As they marched him toward the police station where he faced certain death for being caught outside the ghetto, an extremely tall German officer (Krüger) appeared and asked where they were taking the boy. They replied, "Das ist ein Jude (This is a Jew)." The officer replied, "A Jew? Then give him to me! I know what I will do with him." The police handed him over, and the soldier grabbed Lova by the hand and dragged him away.

After walking a short distance, he stopped, pointed to a door, and tried to explain that it was a church. Lova should go there on Sunday, and the pastor would help him. Lova knocked on the door after the officer left, but there was no answer, so he returned to the ghetto. Many years later, Gerhard Krüger's son got to hear the firsthand story of how his father personally snatched Lova from the hands of death.[14]

Meeting of some of the children who survived the orphanage and Horst Krüger (tall man with tie and vest), Lydia Petrova (second from left), Lova Kravetz (third from the left), and Anatoly Dikushin (fifth from left between Krüger and Lova)

Due to the requirements that Yad Vashem has to identify someone as Righteous Among the Nations, clear, firsthand testimony from those who were saved is required with every detail verified. The Iron Curtain long prevented information from being exchanged between East and West, so many stories from Belarus were never told. Many of the Righteous and those they saved have passed away, and we will never know how many unnamed Righteous Among the Nations there actually were.

One example of this is the village of Porechye located between the cities of Grodno and Minsk. During the last pogrom in the ghetto, about forty children escaped. Since children already had found ways to sneak out of the ghetto to find food, they knew how to escape when the pogrom began. One preferred route was through the large Jewish cemetery that ran along the ghetto's western border, since the Nazis and Polizei did not patrol this area. Maya Krapina was one of these children. Her brother, Joseph, had escaped the ghetto earlier and attempted to join the partisans. After finding partisans near Porechye, he returned to Minsk to rescue Maya. They escaped as the Nazis began the last Aktion in the ghetto. As they fled, they encountered other children trying to escape, and Joseph heroically led forty of them more than 150 km (90 miles) to Porechye. There, the kind-hearted villagers determined that each family would be responsible for one child from this large group.

Maya was taken in by a woman named Anastasia Khurs, who didn't have any children and whose husband was fighting with the partisans. At times, life in the village was almost normal. The villagers made rag dolls for the children, and they could go outside and play. A nearby partisan unit did everything they could to protect the children, often warning them of approaching Nazis or even evacuating them and hiding them in the swamp. Maya and the other children often had to spend several days hiding in the swamp. During the winter, it was brutally cold, but the Germans were afraid to venture into the swamps, so it was relatively safe.

For her role in protecting Maya, Anastasia received the title Righteous Among the Nations in 1994. However, most of the villagers of Porechye did not receive this recognition, since their actions could not be documented according to Yad Vashem's requirements. In 2000, the children who survived because of this village's bravery and compassion constructed a monument in honor of the righteous village of Porechye.

Maya Krapina and Anastasia Khurs

Yaakov

Often it took the actions of those who survived to recognize their rescuers. This was the case with Irina Masyukevich, who sheltered Yaakov Levin and his family. When the Levin family heard about the title of Righteous Among the Nations, they submitted the names of Irina and the village elder, Danila Yurochka, who helped protect them. In 1995, Irina was recognized as Righteous Among the Nations. Yurochka did not receive the award because Yad Vashem determined he did not risk his well-being through the assistance that he offered the family. The Levin family stayed in touch with Irina and remained forever grateful for the sacrifice she made to protect them despite having three children of her own to care for. After her death, Yaakov was sure to lay flowers in her honor at the memorial to the Righteous Among the Nations in Babruysk.

Vladimir

Gratitude for their rescuers is often a defining feature of many of the survivors' stories. Vladimir Sverdlov's story is defined by his gratitude for the woman who saved him and his desire to honor her memory. Throughout his life, he sought to show his respect and gratitude to her in any way that he could.

Vladimir lived in the city of Rogachev before the war with his parents, brother, and grandmother. His father was a Communist Party official in their city, and in the summer of 1941, the family sent eleven-year-old Vladimir to the children's sanatorium in Krynki, near the village of Daraganovo. It was a beautiful place, surrounded by pine trees and situated on the bank of the Ptich River, west of Babruysk. Sanatoriums in the Soviet Union functioned partly as a resort and partly as a medical facility, and it was common for people to go to them.

When the war broke out, Vladimir and most of the other children were trapped at the sanatorium. Hearing of the invasion, many of the staff left, and the older children made their way home. The parents of some of the younger children came to collect them, but the parents of the Jewish children did not. Most had been imprisoned in ghettos so swiftly that they were unable to get their children.

When the Nazis arrived, they shot the woman in charge and turned the sanatorium into a children's ghetto. They sewed yellow patches onto the children's clothes and brought other children from the nearby orphanages. The children were all put to work as slave labor in the fields, harvesting potatoes and other crops.

The guards who ran the makeshift ghetto were not Germans. The commander was a former Red Army major from Ukraine who joined the Nazis after becoming a POW. One female guard was particularly cruel. Any infraction of the rules would result in being locked in an isolation box called "the cooler" for several days. In addition to the solitary confinement that the guards used, a local police officer guarded the children and beat them with a whip made from a metal cable that he carried. Once he caught Vladimir trying to steal food from the garbage and began to beat him with this whip. Vladimir tore off his yellow patch, and this provoked the police officer to give him such a harsh beating that he could not move for days. After the beating, the officer told Vladimir he would have rather shot him, but he did not have the authority to do so.

The pleasant resort turned into a hellish environment. The children received a small amount of bread each day and became so desperate for food they tried to eat the raw, dirt-covered beets, potatoes, and cabbages they harvested.

Vladimir became friends with another boy named Yasha. Yasha was only twelve years old, but since he was the oldest child, he took it upon himself to care for the younger ones. He made everyone break off a little of their bread to share with the weakest children.

Once winter arrived, the conditions got worse. The guards placed all 150 children in one large room. They had no beds and slept on piles of leaves in the freezing cold. They were allowed three pieces of wood to burn each day. If someone put an extra log on the fire, they got three days in the cooler, locked in a box with snow thrown in on top of them. The freezing children huddled together in their summer clothes, since this was all they had to wear. No one had packed winter clothes, and the summer clothes and shoes offered little protection against the brutal Belarussian winter. Many of the children suffered frostbite, and at least one child died almost every night. The guards removed the bodies, and since the ground was frozen, they cut a hole in the ice and threw them into the river. All winter long, the children suffered from fear and despair as their ordeal went on day after day.

One of the few things that punctured the misery of their existence was one young boy named Fima who practiced on his violin every night. At first, this annoyed some of the children, and they told him to stop because they were trying to sleep. Yasha spoke with him about it, and Fima explained he promised his parents that he would practice every night. "If you promised," Yasha said, "then you must keep your word." Fima went on practicing. Sometimes he went outside and wrote musical notes in the snow. One night, the sound of unbelievably beautiful violin music woke the sleeping children, and they saw Fima sitting by the window, playing like they had never heard him play before.

On April 2, some police officers from the nearby village arrived with a German officer and gave the children news that filled them with hope. They were being transferred to another camp where they would get good food and have a nice, cozy place to stay. The children gathered as their names were read off. There were either eighty-two or eighty-four children, including Vladimir, Yasha, and Fima, and several staff members who refused to leave the children throughout their ordeal. In autumn, there had been 150 children, but almost half of them had not survived the winter.

As they marched down the road, surrounded by Belarusian police and Nazi soldiers, Yasha whispered to Vladimir, "Do you think that they are really taking us somewhere nice and warm? Why are all the guards carrying rifles? They are going to kill us." The grim realization hit Vladimir, that Yasha was right. "We should run," he replied. Yasha said, "I look like a stereotypical Jew. They would catch me right away. Plus, I can't leave the little kids." He motioned toward the children clinging to him. He pointed out that Vladimir did not look Jewish and might be able to get away. Vladimir ducked off the road into the thick pine forest and began to run. There were no shots or shouts, but Vladimir kept running, unsure if anyone had noticed him. He injured his leg but did not stop until he collapsed from exhaustion.

When he recovered his strength, he walked through the forest until he found a barn. The owner found him and gave him some milk and bread, the best food he had eaten in months. Seeing his injured leg, the man took him to a village and told him where the doctor lived. Vladimir got lost and could not find the doctor, so he went to a random house and asked for help. The man treated his leg and let him stay for a week to recover. He then sent Vladimir away, warning him that otherwise the police would find him.

It was not until much later that Vladimir discovered the fate of his friends. He heard what happened from locals who witnessed the event. Unlike in western Europe, the Nazis in Soviet territory seldom made any effort to hide their actions and carried them out in broad daylight. Often they forced local people to help by digging graves or sorting the victims' clothing. These methods left thousands of witnesses across the Soviet territories, although many were so shocked by what they had witnessed, they did not speak of it for decades. This was the case in Krynki, where witnesses report seeing the mass grave being dug and the column of children being driven through the village and taken to the pit to be shot. One of the saddest images that Vladimir recalls was how one person remembered seeing a small violin, riddled with bullets, next to the body of the child who clung to it until the last moment of his short life.

Vladimir wandered through the forest for weeks, eating what little he could find until he collapsed from hunger and exhaustion. He awoke surprised to find a Belarusian woman gently shaking him. She asked him if he could walk and, if so, if he would come with her and her daughter. He replied that he could walk to the ends of the earth as long as they did not abandon him in the forest. She took him to her village of Makarichi and told the neighbors that he was a nephew visiting her.

He lived there with the woman, Aleksandra Zvonnik, and her three daughters for the remainder of the war. After she nursed him back to health, he began helping out in the fields, cutting firewood, and caring for the youngest daughter, a two-month-old infant. Aleksandra was only thirty-six years old, but Vladimir, who always found the humor in a situation, affectionately called her Baba (Grandmother) Alesya due to her habit of wearing a headscarf all the time, wrapped tightly to help her cope with chronic migraines.

Baba Alesya

Baba Alesya's care for Vladimir often made her daughters jealous that a stranger their mother found in the woods got the same treatment that they did. Baba Alesya told them, "I'll take care of the stranger, and God will protect my children." A devout Christian, she often prayed and encouraged Vladimir to pray and believe in God. Her example profoundly impacted him, and despite been raised in an atheistic family with Communist Party officials for parents, he began to trust in God. Vladimir maintained a close relationship with her for the rest of her life and never forgot how an Orthodox Christian woman saved him. He did what he could to honor her and her faith at every chance he got. He told his story to Yad Vashem, and due to his efforts, Baba Alesya was recognized as a Righteous Among the Nations in 2004.

For Vladimir, Baba Alesya became like a second mother. For many, the circumstances of war and the Holocaust brought Jewish survivors and their rescuers together in ways that created close relationships that lasted for life. Many actually became family.

Yelena

Such was the case of Yelena Bugayeva, who never knew her birth parents. A hail of bullets from a Nazi submachine gun cut her connection to them when she was an infant.

In the summer of 1941, shortly after the Nazis invaded, a Belarussian woman named Vera Lobatova saw a column of Jewish people being marched down Nemiga Street near the ghetto. A young Jewish woman carrying a baby began to run, trying to escape. A guard opened fire, and the woman and child fell to the ground. Leaving them lying in a pool of blood, the column marched on. Vera approached the still figure and saw that the woman was dead, but she heard a faint cry from underneath the body. She pulled the baby girl out and found that she was alive, although she had a bullet wound in her shoulder. Knowing the risk of hiding a Jewish child as well as realizing she needed medical attention, Vera hid the baby in a basket and took her to her own children's doctor. Dr. Varvara Yanushevich treated the bullet wound and, to prevent the Nazis from finding her, hid her in the hospital for infectious diseases on Kropotkin Street in Minsk. She knew that the Nazis would not come to the hospital for fear they would be exposed to some disease.

Yelena with her adopted mother and rescuer, Varvara Yanushevich

After the baby recovered, Dr. Yanushevich took her home where she and her husband, Mikhail, cared for the child. After the war, they adopted Yelena and raised her as their own. Growing up an only child, Yelena received an abundance of love and attention. If they had told anyone that she was a Jewish child from the ghetto, she would have ended up in an orphanage. After Yelena discovered the truth about her Jewish identity, Varvara and Mikhail Yanushevich received the award of Righteous Among the Nations in 2011.

Alexander

Alexander had lost his entire family in one day when the Einsatzgruppe showed up at their home while he was at orchestra practice. He also found a new family in his rescuers. As he fled from the Einsatzgruppe, he went to a neighbor of his grandparents. The house that he chose belonged to Ksenia Titova, who lived there with her adult daughter, Yevgenia Dombrovskaya, and her teenage granddaughter, Maria. He did not know the family well but remembered one time, before the war, seeing Maria sitting under a tree, playing her guitar. He offered to tune it for her and later said that he felt something about her during that first meeting.

Although he did not know the family, he could only hope they would help him, and they did. He hid in their basement for five months, coming out only at night to eat and get some fresh air. During this time, Maria's nine-year-old cousin came to stay with them, but she learned not to give away the secret about the Jewish boy hiding in the basement. The family supplied the partisans with food, which Maria often delivered, since she could get through checkpoints without being stopped due to her age and beauty. Since they supported the partisans, the family convinced them to accept Alexander into their ranks. Usually partisans accepted only people who could supply their own weapon when they came, but they made an exception for him. Before Alexander left, Maria embroidered a scarf for him, and they bid each other farewell and promised to meet again after the war. Years later, Alexander wrote a song about their story, telling how they fell in love during trying times and how he had to go away to war. In 2015, Maria, her mother, and grandmother were all recognized as Righteous Among the Nations. Maria never considered her actions special or heroic in any way. She felt she did what any caring human being should do.

Any attempt to articulate the full significance of these people's actions will be inadequate. Their bravery, love, and compassion serve as an inspiration and a challenge to all those who find themselves living in dark times.

"In the worst darkness that beset the earth, they lit a candle of righteousness...these people lit candles of truth and humanity in a sea of darkness and we shall forever remember them."
—FORMER PRIME MINISTER OF ISRAEL,
BENJAMIN NETANYAHU[15]

The memory of these people, both victims and rescuers, calls for action. We must remember not only in words but also through our deeds. As hatred, racism, and antisemitism again fill our world, seeking to turn people against the weak and demonize minorities among us, we all have a moral obligation to follow the examples of these brave people. The light of their actions, as Netanyahu said so beautifully, burns before us. These people lived through one of the most terrifying times in human history. They witnessed some of the greatest crimes ever committed, yet they did not let fear or hate overwhelm them. The light in their souls illuminated the plight of their fellow human beings and became a beacon of hope to those lost in the storm and darkness that descended with the Nazis.

All the darkness in the world cannot extinguish the light of one single candle.
—ST. FRANCIS OF ASSISI

CHAPTER 7

Finding the Strength to Rebuild: Coping with the Aftermath

———❦———

The Red Army entered Minsk on July 3, 1944, liberating it after three years of Nazi occupation. Within a month, all of Belarus was back under Soviet control. As quickly as the Nazi hoards had descended, they were gone, driven out by the Soviet forces' relentless efforts to defend their homeland.

The war had taken a terrible toll. Belarus lost the most people of any Soviet Republic. Estimating the number of Jewish victims of the Holocaust in Belarus is more difficult due to incomplete records and the Nazis' effort to conceal their crimes. However, the most common estimate is eight hundred thousand Jewish people. Not only had eight hundred thousand Jewish people died on Belarusian soil (including the Hamburg Jews and refugees from Poland), but one-quarter of the entire Belarusian population—more than 2.2 million people—had perished, double the percentage of anywhere else in the Soviet Union. Thousands of villages were nothing but ashes, and cities like Minsk lay in ruins. With more than 80 percent of its buildings destroyed, the damage to Minsk was so extensive that city planners considered starting over and rebuilding in a different location. In the end, the city stayed in the original spot.

The Soviet ideology that sought to promote equality considered being a Soviet citizen the only important identity. This resulted in a lack of recognition of the Jewish victims whose deaths, in the Soviet perspective, were no different than that of other Soviet citizens who perished fighting for the motherland. The Soviet authorities preferred not to acknowledge the reality that Jewish citizens had been singled out and targeted for extermination by the Nazis.

Some survivors who longed for liberation and the end of the war, but they faced new and unexpected challenges after liberation.

Leonid with his son, Velodia

Leonid

Leonid Rubinstein survived the Minsk Ghetto and concentration camps in Poland, France, and Germany. When the American army arrived and a tank smashed through the fence of Dachau, he found himself free but far from home. He received a card stating he had been liberated from Dachau, and he waited for instructions from the Soviet military. The Americans warned him not to go home because he could be mistreated, but he replied that he wanted to return to his homeland and his family's graves. The Soviets provided transportation for him and the other prisoners to return home, and he set out through Austria, Hungary, and Ukraine. In Austria, his card explaining his liberation from Dachau was taken and not returned.

In Ukraine, he was taken to a camp controlled by the Soviet SMERSH, an acronym that means "Death to Spies." The SMERSH was the Soviet counterintelligence service, and one of its tasks after the war was to examine the prisoners and forced laborers who returned from German captivity. Their suspicion was aroused because Leonid did not have papers explaining that he was liberated from a concentration camp. They asked why he survived while all the other Jews died. After several days, they told him that they had evidence that he had been a collaborator and fought with the Germans. The officer pretended to read from a notebook on his desk. Leonid naively tried to look at it, confused by the information they claimed to have. One of the guards punched him in the face and knocked out several of his teeth. After the pain wore off, he refused to answer their questions and told them, "If I survived multiple concentration camps only to be killed here, just get it over with." Finally, they released him and asked where he wanted to go. He said that although Minsk was his home, everyone he knew there was dead, and he had nowhere to go. He volunteered to join a labor battalion, helping to rebuild damaged cities. Later, he discovered that some relatives had survived, so he returned to Minsk.

Leonid's experience reflected the Soviets' distrust and paranoia toward those who had been in German hands during the war. POWs, officials in occupied areas, and sometimes even partisans fell under suspicion of being German collaborators. There was some reason for concern, since the Nazis recruited some Soviet POWs to fight on their side. However, for the Jewish survivors, it was another challenge. When the question of where they were during the war came up, it led to suspicion if they admitted they had been in a ghetto or otherwise imprisoned.

For many Jewish survivors, rebuilding their shattered lives was challenging, as they no longer had any family support. Their relatives all perished in the Holocaust. The scars and post-traumatic stress disorder (PTSD) the survivors suffered went unacknowledged and untreated. In Belarus in particular, a feeling of being forgotten haunted many survivors. While the stories of the Holocaust in Germany, Poland, and Western Europe became well known and studied, information about what had happened in Belarus remained buried deep behind the Iron Curtain.

In the postwar era, Jewish survivors faced a new series of challenges. Before the war, the Soviet Union made antisemitism illegal, and although it was impossible to outlaw a prejudice, outward acts of hate were uncommon. However, after the war, official attitudes began to change.

Mikhail

Mikhail reflected that he hardly realized he was Jewish until the Nazis came and ordered the Jews into the ghettos. With no involvement in church, synagogue, or mosque due to the Communist restrictions on freedom of worship, many Belarusians did not have a strong identity beyond that of a Soviet citizen. With the Nazis' arrival, antisemitism was encouraged rather than outlawed.

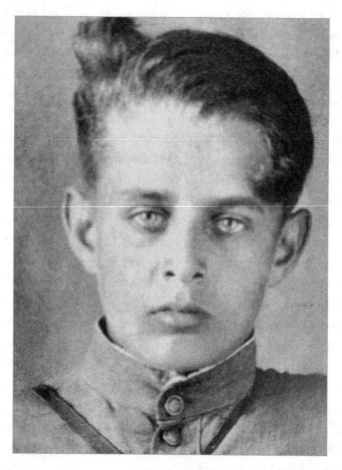

Mikhail in 1944

After the war, antisemitism remained but in a different form. Mikhail succeeded in getting a job as an engineer. By 1968, he was the chief engineer of the Electrical Nets Project Institute, where he encountered a new type of antisemitism institutionalized in the Soviet government.

This antisemitism developed after one of the biggest events in Jewish history: the rebirth of the Nation of Israel on May 14, 1948. The Soviet Union initially viewed the establishment of Israel positively. Three days after Israel announced independence, the Soviet Union became the second nation to recognize the new Jewish state. In the early days of Israel's development, the United States and Europe implemented an arms embargo on the region and would not sell any weapons to the Israelis. Facing the combined might of the armies of their Arab neighbors (equipped with state-of-the-art British weapons), the Israelis began looking for military aid wherever they could find it. Seeing that Israel was a socialist country, the Soviet Union hoped to draw it to the Communist side of the Cold War. It began channeling rifles and aircraft captured during World War II through Communist Czechoslovakia to the Jewish State. In an ironic twist of history, many of the rifles were German Mausers that the Nazis had used. These same weapons helped equip the newly established Israel Defense Forces (IDF).

However, the friendly relationship between Israel and the USSR would not last. As it became clear that Israel chose to ally with the West, the Soviets began to display an anti-Israel perspective.

During this era, Stalin realized that the Jewish identity within the Soviet Union remained strong. Due to the initial goodwill between the Soviet and Israeli governments, Golda Meir went to Moscow on the first official Israeli diplomatic mission in 1948. Thousands of Soviet Jews flooded the streets and packed the synagogue, excited to welcome the first Israeli diplomat to the Soviet Union. Seeing the Soviet Jews identifying so strongly with the State of Israel provoked Stalin's Soviet ideology that sought to suppress nationalistic identity. Soviet propaganda began to rail against "International Zionism" and perpetuate myths of a great Jewish conspiracy to rule the world and destroy the Communist revolution. These ideas drew from the earlier czarist antisemitism based on "Protocols of the Elders of Zion" publications that accused Jews of dishonest exploitation of gentile nations. They even suggested that the

Jewish concept of being the Chosen People was similar to the Nazis' belief in Aryan racial superiority.

Stalin targeted the Jewish Antifascist Committee (JAC), a group of Jewish intellectuals who worked during the war to unite the international community against the Nazis. After the war, their mission shifted to documenting the Holocaust. This challenged the official Soviet position that the Nazis persecuted all Soviet citizens regardless of nationality and race. The Soviets saw the JAC's efforts to record the targeting of Jewish victims as nationalistic activity against the Soviet Union. In 1948, Stalin ordered the assassination of the JAC leader, Solomon Mikhoels. Mikhoels was a Yiddish theater actor in addition to his work with the JAC. While traveling to Minsk for work, he was kidnapped and murdered by the secret police. They dumped his body in the street and drove over it with a truck to make it appear that he had been the victim of a hit-and-run accident.

Soon after this, thirteen other members of the JAC (many of whom were Yiddish-speaking poets and actors) were arrested and given a sham trial. On August 12, 1952, "The Night of the Murdered Poets," they were executed.

A Jewish doctor named Yakov Etinger was also arrested and tortured to death. Dr. Etinger had briefly treated Stalin's heir apparent, Andrei Zhdanov, who died from heart failure in 1948. This death inspired a conspiracy theory that the Soviets created, claiming that Jewish doctors were plotting to murder high-ranking Soviet officials.

The Soviets began a campaign to arrest the supposed "killer doctors" whom they claimed worked for the Americans. They arrested thirty-seven prominent physicians, many of whom were Jewish, between 1951 and early 1953 as part of this "Doctors' Plot." Stalin's reputation for brutally murdering anyone he saw as a threat to his power and the fact that millions were victims of his paranoid political purges in the 1930s made it entirely possible that he intended another major purge. It is almost unimaginable that the Soviet Jewish population, which was still recovering from the Holocaust, could have faced another attempt to destroy it. The construction of large camps in Kazakhstan and Siberia at the time ominously suggest that Stalin may have intended to deport and imprison the entire Jewish population. On March 1, 1953, the Jewish people celebrated the holiday of Purim, a reminder of God's deliverance from a genocidal regime. That night, Stalin was found unconscious on his bedroom floor. He had apparently suffered from a stroke and died a few days later. The Soviet government admitted that the Doctors' Plot was a fabrication and dropped all charges. After Stalin's death, the brutal murders and torture ended.

By 1967, the Soviets supported Egypt and Syria in the Six-Day War against Israel. After a surprise Israeli victory, the USSR's relationship with the Israelis worsened, because the Soviets saw their allies' defeat as a blot on their influence in the region. This embarrassment led to a return of anti-Zionist propaganda and repression yet in a less violent form.

Against this historical backdrop, Mikhail Treister received an "invitation" to visit the feared KGB (Soviet secret police) headquarters in Minsk in the autumn of 1968. He did not know the reason for the invitation but knew one of his coworkers, a fellow Jew named Leopold, had recently been arrested. The foreman informed everyone that he was suspected of crimes under the "jurisdiction of national security." Mikhail knew what this meant. After the Israeli victory in the Six-Day War, a little over a year before, Leopold took a new interest in Israel. He began collecting books and information, and in his naive zeal, he began sharing them with his Jewish friends and coworkers.

Mikhail reflected on all of this as he arrived at the massive KGB building in the center of Minsk. This location boasts the largest façade of any building in the city, inspiring a feeling of intimidation surpassed only by what people knew took place behind the tall wooden doors. As Mikhail entered, he found himself in a large, empty lobby. A voice from above greeted him. Looking up, he saw a KGB lieutenant colonel leaning on the banister of the second floor, waiting for him. Once they reached the investigator's office, the interrogation began oddly. Inspector Gorshkov asked Mikhail if he needed an interpreter. Mikhail wittily replied that if the officer intended to ask questions in Yiddish or Hebrew, an interpreter would be needed, but as long as the conversation remained in Russian, he would be fine. The interrogation lasted three hours, addressing what Mikhail knew of his coworker's activities and if he had been given books. Afterward, Mikhail was released until his coworker's trial. After being required to testify as a witness, the government concluded that no harm resulted from reading "unapproved" books, so they released the defendant and the witnesses.

Although he was innocent, Mikhail faced repercussions. The next day, he arrived at work only to be taken aside and informed that the government had revoked his security clearance. This meant that his project of designing electrical lines could not be completed, as it required the use of classified topographical maps.

Mikhail's career suffered even further as he was informed that he was going to be demoted. He and several other Jewish employees, who experienced similar actions, all submitted letters of resignation.

As he sought another job, Mikhail found that news about these events had spread, and it was difficult to find a place that would risk trouble with the Communist Party by hiring him. After a great deal of effort, he finally found work in his field again.

Mikhail's experiences were not unique. Many Jewish people were denied employment and educational opportunities. Jews often looked for ways to hide their identity. Their name often gave them away, so they attempted to change it or marry a Russian or Belarusian. An even harder issue to address was that all passports recorded ethnic identity, and all Jewish persons had the word "Jew" printed in their documents.

The Soviet opposition to Zionism found a new form of persecution when many Soviet Jews saw immigration to Israel as a means of escape. The Soviet Union began severely limiting Jewish emigration, citing security concerns that Jewish engineers would share Soviet secrets with the West.

One needed an exit permit to leave the Soviet Union to make *aliyah* (immigrate to Israel). It became standard policy that as soon as someone applied for an exit permit, they lost their job. No longer able to work in their field and waiting for exit permits that were usually not granted, they faced the prospect of being labeled a "social parasite." It was considered a crime to be unemployed for two months or longer, since unemployed people were seen as a burden to Soviet society. Many took any job they could find including street-sweeper and other jobs far below their qualification levels. These Soviet Jews were called "Refuseniks," and their plight became an example of Soviet violations of human rights. Often arrested and interrogated by the KGB, the Refuseniks struggled to survive and waited to be free. Although international pressure led to the gradual easing of emigration requirements in the 1970s, most Soviet Jews were not able to make aliyah until the Soviet Union collapsed in 1991.

In addition to the perceived political threat of Zionism that led to many anti-Jewish activities, atheistic values motivated Soviets to suppress many Jewish customs with a religious origin.

For the survivors whose stories you have read in these pages, the suffering and trials did not end with liberation. They all carried trauma and scars from the Holocaust for the remainder of their lives. Many were haunted by the question of why they survived while their loved ones did not. It is a question without an answer. Some found themselves facing difficult situations living under Communism while they tried to rebuild the normal life that the Nazis stole from them. Many found strength and purpose in serving alongside their fellow survivors or preserving the memory of those who were lost or the righteous ones who acted on their behalf. Others felt that after what they and their families experienced, the situation under the Soviets was like living in paradise.

Yaakov

Yaakov, Misha, and their mother survived the war together. She got a job as a bookkeeper and found an apartment. Their neighbor, Paperny Moiseivich Wolfe, a disabled war veteran wounded in the Battle of Stalingrad, began to help the young widow and boys, and he told the young family that he loved them with all his heart. His family had been killed in Bulgaria, and after some time, he and Yaakov's mother got married. The family moved to Minsk, where Yaakov's stepfather found work. However, they lived in the poverty that many suffered in the Soviet era.

They lived on ration cards under the Soviet Communist system. One day, they sent Misha to get bread. He waited in line all day, and when he finally reached the service window, they closed for the day. A man nearby told him that he knew someone who worked there, and he could help. Misha gave him the ration cards, and the man left. He never returned, having deceived the eight-year-old and stolen the family's food rations. That month, the family had almost no food.

Yaakov studied to be a technician and got a job at the tractor factory in Minsk. At one point, tractors were Belarus's primary export, and the government-run factories proved vital to the economy. Yaakov's manager offered him a position as a supply chief. However, when he sought approval from the government, they rejected Yaakov since he was Jewish.

Sima after the war

Sima

After the war, Sima was alone and unsure of the fate of her father, who joined the partisans at the beginning of the war. In July 1944, the Soviet liberators organized a parade to honor the partisans who fought the Nazi occupation for so many years. More than thirty thousand partisans attended. To her astonishment, Sima spotted her father in the crowd, leading to a joyful yet bittersweet reunion as he learned that the rest of the family had perished in the ghetto.

Yelena

For Yelena and her adopted parents, the postwar era proved to be difficult. They knew if anyone found out Yelena was a Jewish orphan and not their daughter, she would be forcefully taken to an orphanage. To prevent this, they left Minsk and moved to the Grodno region near the Polish border. They distanced themselves from everyone who knew them before the war. After several years, they obtained a birth certificate from the village council, listing them as her parents. Yelena grew up with these loving parents, never knowing the dark past that brought them together. They raised her in the Russian Orthodox Church, and she learned the Lord's Prayer at a young age. Her father came from a family of priests and studied in a seminary before the war, but he was unable to pursue his plan to become a priest because the Communists outlawed religion. Her mother continued to serve as a village doctor, often rushing off in the night to attend to those who needed her care. Her father became an academic advisor in the field of agriculture.

Yelena with her rescuer and adoptive mother, Varvara Yanushevich

As she got older, Yelena's classmates began to notice she looked nothing like her parents and had Jewish features. They targeted her with slurs on the playground. She began asking her parents about this subject after a cousin hinted that she may not be their child. Her mother denied it all, fearing the truth would impact Ylena's love for her, and she responded that Yelena should ignore people's fantasies. When Yelena graduated from college, one of her cousins told her she was Jewish, but still her mother denied it. Later, a Jewish friend of her mother confirmed this fact and told her they rescued her from the ghetto. When she asked her mother again, Varvara forbade Yelena from ever bringing up the subject again. However, on her deathbed, she admitted the truth.

Yelena told her that this did not change the fact that she was her mother and she loved her even more now that she knew the sacrifice that they made to adopt her. Only after finding out the truth about her past did Yelena solve a question that often puzzled her: what caused the unexplained scar on her shoulder? After hearing the details of her rescue, she realized it was the gunshot wound that caused her rescuer to bring her to a doctor—who later became her adoptive mother.

Raisa

After the war, Raisa and Vera's mother took them back to their old house only to find it in ruins. She attempted to get the girls into school, but the tuition was too much for her to pay. Faced with these desperate circumstances, she resorted to the only course of action she could think of. She had survived the war through great daring, and if they hoped to survive in the inhospitable postwar Soviet Union, she needed to continue to take daring risks. She wrote a letter to Stalin, explaining the situation she faced with her young girls. The letter reached someone in the government who assisted them, and soon they received government housing and access to school.

Raisa and her mother attempted to hide the full horror of what they had experienced from Vera, who was a sensitive child. Eventually they revealed what they had endured during the war.

Raisa (on left) with a friend while studying at university in 1956

After she grew up, Vera left Belarus and moved to Estonia. Raisa got married and attended Mogilev Technical Training College. While at university, one of Raisa's teachers was Wolf Messing. He was a Polish Jew and professed to be a psychic. Raisa had an interest in spiritual things, but since religion was banned in the USSR, she began exploring supernatural ideas through his teaching. After graduating in 1957, she began working as a kindergarten teacher in Minsk.

When she got older, her husband passed away, leaving her a childless widow. Vera remained her only family, but since she lived in Estonia, they could not see each other easily. After the USSR collapsed, they could speak only by phone. Both sisters were lonely, carrying the scars of what they experienced in the Holocaust. Although these events happened many years before, the scars and trauma remained. Vera insists that "time does not heal" the grief and pain they suffered.

Alexander

For Alexander, who spent years fighting the Nazis as a partisan, the liberation of Mogilev meant he had a chance to track down the neighbor who had betrayed his family to the Nazis. He found the man in pain and dying from cancer. Rather than taking revenge, Alexander felt sorry for him and felt that God had judged him by inflicting him with a painful and fatal illness.

Alexander and Maria

Alexander also hoped to be reunited with his love, Maria, and her family. However, he found their village had been burned, and it was some time before he found out where they had gone. When he reunited with Maria and her mother, everyone was filled with joy and relief. Maria's grandmother passed away during the war, but Maria and her mother were overjoyed that Alexander had survived. Alexander and Maria's feelings for each other had not decreased despite the years they were separated by the war. Soon after being reunited, they got married and began a family of their own. Alexander built a house for his new family while working three jobs. They had three daughters who he named in honor of his murdered sisters: Zoya, Tamara, and Larisa. He believed that God gave him three girls to replace his three sisters. They raised their girls with a strong connection to their father's Jewishness. Even though she was not Jewish, Maria could speak Yiddish better than Alexander and cook traditional Jewish dishes, skills she learned living near many Jewish neighbors.

Alexander devoted his postwar life to his passion for music. Since he could no longer play the violin because of the wounds he suffered during the war, he became one of the best accordionists in the city. He started teaching in 1944 at a music college in Mogilev, a role he would continue for the next forty-five years. He was most proud of having his work depicted in Mogilev's encyclopedia and the recognition his students and choirs received.

For his military service, he received the Order of the Patriotic War, the Red Star, and the Partisan of the Patriotic War medals.

Zoya

After spending a year in the orphanage, Zoya enrolled in a vocational school at a radio plant and spent the next three years training there. She was happy to have survived and found a place to live and earn some money. She learned to sew and knit and knitted or sewed when she got home from the plant. In 1993, former ghetto prisoners and concentration camp victims formed an organization of more than 350 survivors. They elected Zoya to be on the leadership council, where she still works as a volunteer.

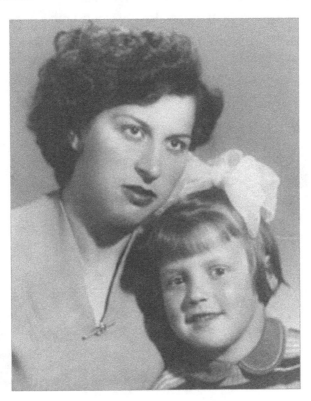

Zoya with her daughter, Margarita

Vladimir

Vladimir left Baba Alesya's home and began looking for his family and opportunities to study. He did not have any identification papers, which made getting into school difficult. In his hometown of Rogachev, people told him that if his family was Jewish, they had been shot. He found work in western Belarus and studied in a technical school to become a welder and blacksmith.

In 1947, he returned to Rogachev and attempted to get new identification documents. The official asked him if his name was Vladimir. Vladimir was surprised that the official knew his name and even more surprised to discover that his father was alive and had searched for him for more than two years. His family now lived in the village of Berezino near Minsk, and it took him almost three days to make the journey. When he arrived, his father hugged him so tightly he almost suffocated. His return shocked his mother so much that she could not speak for half an hour.

After spending some time with his family, Vladimir wished to introduce them to Baba Alesya, whom he considered a second mother. When they met, his father repeatedly thanked her for protecting and caring for his son, but being a humble woman, she did not think she had done anything to merit such gratitude. Vladimir often visited her to do everything he could for her, including installing electricity in her house and replacing her roof.

Vladimir with his wife, Maria, and his son, Vasilli

Vladimir became a skilled and highly sought-after metalworker. Often priests hired him to design and craft crosses to adorn church steeples. Knowing Baba Alesya was a devout Christian and seeing her example of faith in God motivated him, and he was proud of each piece he created for a church. Every cross that he made, he did in honor of her.

Vladimir at the memorial to the children of Krynki

As the lone survivor of the Krynki Sanatorium, Vladimir felt a duty to honor and preserve the memory of his friends who perished. He made it his mission to erect a memorial on the site. He found the district officials sympathetic, but they did not have money in the budget for such a project. Vladimir saved part of his meager pension and paid for the costs himself. On October 27, 2006, the monument was unveiled with the simple inscription in Yiddish and Belarusian: "To the memory of the 84 Jewish children from the sanatorium of Krynki, shot by the Nazis in April 1942."

Irina

After the war, Irina and her siblings were reunited with their aunt. The daughter of Anna Shipro (the member of the underground who smuggled them out of the ghetto) found their aunt and explained how her mother had rescued the children from the ghetto and placed them in Orphanage Number 2 under false names. Hearing this, Irina's aunt found the starving, ill, and traumatized children and took them out of the orphanage. She also located their oldest brother who had been away at summer camp when the war began. He had been evacuated, and after the war, he returned to Belarus, found his siblings, and learned of his parents' fate. After the war, Irina discovered that after her family had been forced into the ghetto, the underground had used their home as the location for a secret printing press. There they had printed the resistance newspaper *Zvezda,* which played an important role of informing people of the Red Army's progress and gave people hope to survive.

Irina got married in 1968 and had a daughter. Although her marriage did not last, she found great joy in raising her little girl. However, the vivid and painful memories of the childhood that had been stolen continued to haunt her.

Lydia

For Lydia, being orphaned was only the beginning of a difficult life and several tragedies. Without any support system or family, her dream of attending university was not possible. She moved to Latvia where she could attend a vocational sewing school. After graduating from this program in 1956, she went to work as a seamstress in Siberia. There she met her husband, and they had two children. She still desired to study, and with her husband's support, she graduated from medical school. In 1973, tragedy struck when her husband died in a mining accident. As a widow with two children, she struggled to provide by working as an X-ray technician. Later, she remarried and moved back to Minsk.

While in Minsk in the late 1980s and early 90s, Lydia felt alone, and she struggled with the reality that she did not have relatives there. She often thought of her adult children who had not returned to Minsk with her. She reconnected with the daughters of Anton Ketsko, the pastor who oversaw the orphanage that hid her from the Nazis during the war.

Anatoly

Anatoly left the orphanage and found his father, who had disappeared before the war. His father had remarried, and Anatoly did not want to live with him and this new stepmother, so he joined the military. Later, he married and had two children.

Anatoly during his military service in the Soviet Navy
(in center with hand on his shoulder)

Lev

Lev finally got to use his degree after the war and became a math teacher. He taught mathematics at the Minsk Radio Engineering College and, in 1968, and received the distinguished title of Honored Teacher of Belarus. He married Nina, a professor of chemistry who taught at Minsk University, and they enjoyed sixty-eight years of marriage. Their son, Ganady, became a professor of medicine and director of the Republic Scientific and Practical Center of Pulmonology and Tuberculosis in Minsk. Lev's father's dream of a good education for his son, which led to their leaving the shtetl, produced generations of academic achievement.

Lev and Nina

As the decades passed, the children of the Holocaust grew older, retired, and watched their children grow into adulthood. Their memories lingered, waiting for a listening ear to hear of their suffering. However, due to the Cold War, much of the world had never heard their stories. As the Iron Curtain collapsed, they would finally get the opportunity to share the accounts of the suffering they endured.

CHAPTER 8

The Curtain Falls: Seeing God Move in Post-Soviet Belarus

⸺ ⸙ ⸺

The US presidential election of 1980 brought the victory of Ronald Reagan, whose hardline policy against appeasement brought a more hostile tone to the Cold War between the USSR and the United States. As a renewed arms race began, no one could have guessed that the Soviet Union would collapse in a little more than a decade.

We believe that God, who knows the future, was preparing us for the role He had for us among the Holocaust survivors in the aftermath of the fall of the Soviet Empire. The year after Reagan's election, we encountered an organization led by a Jewish follower of Yeshua (Jesus) who survived imprisonment and persecution in Communist Romania. Through hearing the experiences of Pastor Richard Wurmbrand, our hearts were moved with compassion for those suffering behind the Iron Curtain, and we looked for ways to help. We donated to organizations including Wurmbrand's that sought to support people of faith who were being persecuted behind the Iron Curtain.

We received reports of how these organizations were helping the hurting people of the Soviet Union while sharing the good news of God's love with them. Knowing that their government denied their citizens the Bible and a knowledge of God, our concern for them increased, especially for those persecuted for their faith. We never dreamed that God had more in store for us than financially supporting and praying for the Jewish and Christian people suffering under Communism.

The Soviet leader Mikhail Gorbachev had attempted a series of political reforms that proved ineffective. Realizing his power was waning and seeing the various Soviet republics agitating for independence, he gave a televised speech on December 25, 1991, declaring the dissolution of the USSR. The hammer and sickle flag was lowered, and the Soviet Union no longer existed. The Soviet Union's attempts to craft an atheistic worldview and proclaim the virtues of the great Soviet society had come to a sudden end. After more than seventy years of being subjected to carefully crafted propaganda and indoctrination, the people of the former Soviet Union faced a void in their worldview as they realized much of what they had been told for decades was not true. In the ideological vacuum, many people felt discouraged and lost and were searching for answers.

This situation in the former Soviet Union gave us our first chance to do more than donate and pray. A friend of ours, Jonathan Bernis, was organizing a Messianic Jewish festival in Belarus, and he invited us to join him. In 1994, much of the world had never heard of Belarus (also called Belorussia or White Russia), which, as you may recall from chapter 1, had often been ruled by other kingdoms and empires.

As we prepared for our short-term trip to Belarus, I (Stewart) thought about how during my childhood in New York City, we had "duck and cover" drills, hiding under our desks in case the Soviets attacked. Now, my wife and I were going to serve the people we had been taught to fear!

Even before leaving for Minsk, I (Chantal) had a deep sense that our life was about to take a dramatic turn. A year before at a Messianic Jewish conference, while hearing Jonathan talking about the needs of the Jewish people in the former Soviet Union, the Lord spoke clearly to my heart that we would move to that part of the world. Now that we were preparing to go on this short-term trip, there was a big question in my heart. Would the Lord make His plan for our future clear during the trip?

At the festival, we witnessed firsthand the tremendous interest these people had in the outside world and anything related to Biblical spirituality. All five nights of the festival, the hall of 4,500 seats was filled, and another five thousand were outside, hoping to get in. It was astonishing to see so many people seeking truth, and thousands of them were Jewish!

During the nine days we spent in Minsk, we connected with many people who were attending the festival. We were treated to amazing Ashkenazi Jewish hospitality, as some of them invited us to share a meal in their small, Soviet-era apartments. We listened intently to their stories and shared about our life in America. They also asked many questions about our faith and beliefs. They told us stories of Soviet propaganda that depicted many Americans living in cardboard boxes. The government had said that this was the sad life for people living with the results of capitalism. Realizing that this propaganda was false, one person ruefully remarked that "it seemed the Soviet authorities had lied about everything." This realization motivated many to explore everything that had been denied to them, foremost of which was information about God and the Bible.

Many of the people we met begged us to return to teach them more from the Bible and explain why we believed Yeshua was the Messiah of Israel. They hungered to know more about how He changed our lives and how He could change theirs for the better. I (Chantal) experienced something I never had before or have since. My heart physically hurt when I thought of leaving these people. God was giving Stewart and me huge compassion for the Jewish people of Belarus. By the time our plane landed in New York, we had made up our minds to move to Belarus to live among them.

It was not an easy decision. Our parents and three of our four children were not pleased. Our Russian-speaking friends in America tried to dissuade us, telling us how they had fled the Soviet Union and asking why we would want to take our family there. They told us how life was so much better in America! We replied that we believed God wanted us to go and serve the Jewish people.

Many of our friends in the United States struggled to understand why the Jewish people of Belarus did not make aliyah and immigrate to Israel. In fact, many did. In the 1990s, the Israeli Ministry of Immigration Absorption estimated seventy-six thousand Belarusian Jews (part of more than a million people from the entire former Soviet Union) made aliyah to Israel in one of the largest waves of immigration in the history of the Jewish state. We were awed to witness what we believed was a fulfillment of something foretold in the Tanakh by the Prophet Jeremiah: "Behold I bring them from the north country and gather them from the uttermost ends of the earth, the blind and the lame amongst them, the woman with child and she who travails with child all together; a great company shall they return there" (Jeremiah 31:7).[16] In fact, after arriving in Belarus, we saw part of this massive ingathering of Jewish people from the "north country" to Israel. At one point, we even found ourselves on a plane packed with people who chose to leave everything behind to go home to the Holy Land. Some were brought aboard on stretchers, vividly fulfilling the prophecy that even the lame would be brought back.

Although making aliyah was a dream come true for many, it was not possible for everyone. For many elderly Holocaust survivors, the prospect of moving to a place where they had never been was frightening. They would have to leave everything and almost everyone they had ever known behind. The challenges of moving with only a couple of suitcases of belongings, and having to adjust to a different culture and language as well as the hot, Middle Eastern climate, were too much for many.

We knew that although many Jewish people were returning home to Israel, we would find many more who chose to remain in post-Soviet Belarus.

We understood that we were entering a country facing great challenges and uncertainties. The country was still reeling from the fallout from the 1986 nuclear reactor explosion at Chernobyl, Ukraine, located 15 km (less than 10 miles) from the Belarusian border. It is estimated that 70 percent of the fallout settled in Belarus, contaminating more than 23 percent of the country, including much valuable farmland.[17] This disaster, and the collapse of the Soviet economy, caused a massive food shortage. In addition to serious health concerns due to the radiation levels, people had to contend with not being able to find enough food. The simultaneous breakdown of the Soviet Union meant the country's infrastructure was crumbling, and the people were experiencing serious financial difficulties. When we arrived with our family in 1995, the average income was about $80 per month—not enough to live on, especially if one was trying to raise a family. Most lost their life savings and pensions because of the collapse of the Soviet Union. People were confused and in despair. Many were depressed, and alcohol and suicide rates were high compared to the rest of the world.[18]

In addition to all these concerns, we were not sure if the government would permit us to stay long term. We didn't speak Russian at the time, which created a daunting language barrier, since only a few Belarusians spoke English. We also wondered how the Jewish community would receive us and how people would feel about our belief that Yeshua was the promised Messiah of Israel spoken of in the Tanakh. Despite the uncertainties we faced, we had an inner sense that things would work out, and we were determined to make the move to Minsk.

As we prepared to move to Belarus, my (Stewart) father shared a bit of history about the Winograd family that I had not known. He informed me that my great-grandmother had come from Belarus. The realization that I had a personal connection to the country and was returning to a place my ancestors had called home was a surprise that impacted me greatly. My excitement to get on the plane that would take us to our new life assignment only increased!

After settling into our new home in Minsk, we began meeting with Felix Lipsky and Mikhail Canterovich, the leaders of the National Association of Holocaust Survivors (mentioned earlier in describing our first Shabbat in Belarus). They introduced us to other members of the association's leadership. When we arrived with our children (Joshua, fourteen, Miriam, thirteen, Sarah, eleven, and David, nine) in tow, the first questions the leaders of the survivors association asked were why we left the United States and what we were doing in Minsk.

We explained that motivated by the love of God, we moved to Belarus so that we could be of help to the Jewish people in this land. We were there to serve them and be their friends, and we would ask for nothing in return. It was apparent they were skeptical and would wait to see if our actions matched our words.

One could say that at our first meeting with the leaders of the Holocaust survivors in 1995, our Comfort for Holocaust Survivors Initiative was born. For more than twenty-six years, we have been faithful to those words we spoke, and as a result, hundreds of survivors saw they could trust us, and many became dear friends.

Mikhail

Shortly after we arrived, Felix Lipsky moved away, and we were introduced to his replacement, Mikhail Treister. Our relationship with him developed into one of our dearest friendships. We worked alongside him and Mikhail Canterovich during our efforts to distribute aid to the survivors of Belarus.

Any uneasiness and skepticism that the National Association of Holocaust Survivors leaders initially felt about us vanished and had been replaced with trust and respect.

Some years later, a few members of the Jewish community asked Mikhail why he was working with Messianic believers and suggested it might be better to keep some distance from us. Mikhail responded, "During the war, the Nazis tried to control me and could not. After the war, the Communists tried to tell me what to believe, but they failed. Now, I am certainly not going to be told how to behave or who I can or cannot be friends with. Stewart and Chantal are my friends! They do more than anyone else to help the Holocaust survivors here in Belarus."

Soon after arriving and seeing the hardships that people faced due to the ongoing economic crisis, we looked for ways to help. Together with Annette Powledge, who came to Belarus with her husband, John, and son, Russel, to work alongside us for a few years, we began organizing a shipment of humanitarian aid. Good friends in the United States, Charles and Rebecca Moody, gathered the supplies. Since the need was so great, this shipment would be the first of many. Within a few years, our efforts exceeded anything we expected. I (Chantal) found myself overseeing numerous shipments of clothing, food, and personal care items from the United States and Europe every year. In those early years, this ongoing, practical expression of our love and care for the survivors caused our friendships and connections to grow deeper.

The economic situation in Belarus gradually stabilized. After Belarus gained independence, Alexander Lukashenko was elected in 1994 as the first (and, as of this writing, only) president. Lukashenko had been a director of a collective farm before entering politics. While Russia and many other former Soviet states went through a fairly rapid process of decentralization that sought to dismantle the Communist government's ownership of industry and production, President Lukashenko took a different approach. He maintained state control of the banks, industry, and economy in a Soviet style. On one hand, this prevented the massive corruption that developed in other former Soviet Republics where oligarchs exploited the process of privatization to seize vast business holdings and dramatically increase their personal wealth. On the other hand, Lukashenko's efforts to maintain a Soviet-style economy led to stagnation.

His hybrid economic approach can be seen reflected in Belarusian architecture, where ultramodern buildings stand beside Soviet-era symbols such as the statue of Lenin. Lukashenko's strong hand controlling the nation led to tension between his government and many Belarusians who demanded a more democratic government. Lukashenko's regime has also had a tense relationship with the Western nations that seek to promote democratic and human rights reforms in Belarus.

Despite the economic and political challenges, the spiritual hunger of the people of Belarus was not quenched. People wanted answers, and God was moving in the hearts of the Jewish and Slavic people through many new congregations, ministries, and Bible studies that had sprung up across the country.

CHAPTER 9

The Candles Burn:
Faith Ignited

You, Lord, keep my lamp burning; my God
turns my darkness into light.

—PSALM 18:28[19]

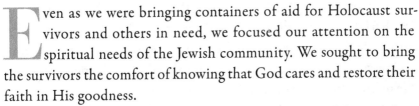

ven as we were bringing containers of aid for Holocaust survivors and others in need, we focused our attention on the spiritual needs of the Jewish community. We sought to bring the survivors the comfort of knowing that God cares and restore their faith in His goodness.

"For the first time in my life, I feel proud to be Jewish." To explain the full implication of this statement, we return to the stories of our friends, the survivors.

The Jewish people of Belarus and the Soviet Union experienced two major tragedies in the twentieth century: The Nazis tried to destroy their lives, families, and communities, and the Soviets attempted to destroy their culture, faith, and connection to their God-given Jewish identity. Through spending time with Holocaust survivors and being invited by their leadership team to teach them about traditional Jewish holidays, the Bible, the God of Israel, and the promised Messiah, we hoped to bring about a degree of restoration.

We have often seen how our work has helped connect survivors with the Jewish identity and faith many had lost. At one of our

Shabbat services, upon hearing Hebrew being sung, one of the survivors remembered the prayers he heard his grandfather pray when he was a boy. Over the years, many survivors who had never prayed before told us they now prayed every morning and at different times throughout the day.

Yaakov

One of the most remarkable examples of this restored Jewish identity and faith in God was our dear friend Yaakov. His grandparents had been religious, but he had never understood what this meant.

Yaakov was one of the leaders of the National Association of Holocaust Survivors, and our relationship with him developed through our monthly meetings with the leadership where we played music, enjoyed a nice meal, and discussed questions of life. We shared from the Bible and answered deep questions that were on the survivors' hearts. Many said that when they came to these meetings, their souls felt comforted and at peace. We considered this a wonderful answer to prayer, as we and our team members regularly prayed that God would bring them comfort. As it is written in Isaiah 51:12: "I, I am the One who comforts you."[20] Indeed, even before arriving in Belarus we sensed Yeshua impressing on our hearts, "you love and serve, expect nothing in return, as this will create opportunities for Me to bring the survivors comfort by My Spirit."

One day, Yaakov told us that he had been impressed by the fact that we desired to help those who suffer. He was struck by the atmosphere of kindness and care in which our team gave people hope by helping them see that God cares and is always near.

The Spirit of God was doing deep work in Yaakov's heart. He eventually became a follower of Yeshua and a key member of the Messianic Jewish Congregation, Brit Chadasha, that we started in Minsk. Brit Chadasha means "new covenant," referencing a passage in Jeremiah 31:31 where God promises the Jewish people a new covenant.

After joining the congregation, Yaakov's desire to help others grow in their relationship with God caused him to open his home to host a Bible study group. He often traveled with us across Belarus, encouraging Jewish people to have faith in the God of Israel and sharing how Yeshua gave him a new beginning, comfort, joy, and purpose. His faith in Yeshua and his active participation in our Messianic Jewish community caused him to proclaim that "this congregation has become my second family, my mishpocha. I had never read the Bible, but now it has become my book for everyday life. It has everything that a person needs in good times and in trouble and for the first time in my life, I feel proud to be Jewish!" He often expressed his appreciation for our congregation's focus on meeting the needs of Holocaust survivors and that many fellow survivors were attending services and having the opportunity to share their memories with younger generations. Yaakov met his beautiful Jewish wife, Tamara, in the congregation. After many years of actively serving the Jewish community, Yaakov passed away in October 2021 at the age of eighty-six during the COVID-19 pandemic. We miss him greatly, but we are confident that he has been reunited with his beloved wife, and is rejoicing in the presence of God.

Yaakov with Stewart and Chantal

Yaakov, his wife, Tamara, our team member, Roman,
and Mikhail Treister during a visit to Auschwitz

Zoya

Zoya also served as a leader of the National Association of Holocaust Survivors with whom we developed a close, family-like relationship. She attended our monthly meetings with the leadership team. We often visited her home where we were guaranteed a banquet of Ashkenazi Jewish cooking as well as a banquet of friendship and fellowship. No one makes gefilte fish as delicious as hers! She often tells us how much she loves our team members and how their love has influenced her.

Zoya and Chantal

Zoya with our team member, Vitalik

Over the years, she shared with Tanya Gamburg, the coordinator of our Comfort for Holocaust Survivors Initiative, that she was so encouraged by the much-needed clothing, food, medicine, and personal care items that we brought into the country. She was impressed by how we provided aid for schools and hospitals and how we cared for orphans and the poor.

Zoya had grown up as an atheist under Communism and was taught that religion was the opium of the masses, but even the Holocaust and seventy years under Communism did not quench her spiritual thirst. She was interested to learn what the Bible said about God, life, and the Jewish holidays and traditions. She realized the good works we were doing in the country, and the love and care she was experiencing through us and our team, were a direct result of our relationship with Yeshua. Her studies of the Bible, our close relationship with her, and the love she experienced from our team led her to decide that what the Bible says about the Messiah is true. She has become a real woman of faith, encouraging others to believe in the God of Israel and embrace Yeshua as the promised Jewish Messiah. She relates to Yeshua with such affection as evidenced by something she often says, "I am on a journey of spiritual growth as I seek to follow after *my* Yeshua." When looking back, she shares how she sees many events in her life as examples of how God protected her.

Zoya is not the only atheist who found a new connection with her Jewishness and the God of Israel. The story of Yevsay Shuster, another survivor who was dear to us, is a powerful example of a Jewish atheist who came to believe in God. Though we did not mention him earlier in this book, we tell his story here due to the amazing transformation that we witnessed in his life.

Yevsay

Yevsay's story of survival is different from others in this book. Although Minsk was his hometown, he was not in Belarus when the Nazis invaded. He was born in 1921, three years after World War I had ended and the Soviets took power through the Bolshevik Revolution. He grew up in the new atheist Soviet State, yet he remembered seeing his grandparents observing the Shabbat while he was a child. The rest of his family was secular, and he was raised as an atheist.

As a child, he showed great artistic promise, and his family wanted to enroll him in a prestigious art school in Vitebsk (the hometown of the renowned Jewish artist Marc Chagall). They could not buy him good clothes to wear to school, so he was unable to attend. Instead, he got a job with the Communist Party as a designer of patriotic posters and other propaganda.

*Yevsay and Stewart (holding a photo of Yevsay
when he was in the military)*

He joined the army and became a naval aviator, flying seaplanes. An often-overlooked story of the Holocaust is the large number of Jewish soldiers who served during the war. Many, like Yevsay, proved to be brave and valuable members of the Soviet and Allied forces and were decorated for their service. When the Nazis attacked, Yevsay was deployed to the vital port of Murmansk on the Arctic Ocean. This port was one of the few that the Soviet Union had access to, and it was the lifeline for the supplies and weapons the Allied forces of the United States and Britain gave the Soviet Union under the Lend-Lease Program. These convoys of ships were often attacked by U-boats (submarines) and the Luftwaffe as they tried to reach Murmansk. It was a dangerous region with frigid weather and heavy fighting.

Yevsay distinguished himself when a Soviet plane crashed into the freezing water. He rescued five of his comrades from the downed plane. In recognition of his daring rescue, a general awarded him an engraved revolver. After the war, he had to turn in this weapon, but it was replaced by a replica made of crystal that was one of his most prized possessions.

Yevsay with his treasured crystal pistol

He returned to Minsk after the war, unsure if he would find any of his family still alive. He was relieved to discover that his father and brothers had survived the war. He began to rebuild his life and met his wife, Valentina, and they had two daughters, Ida and Rita. He continued to work as an artist for the government and even helped design the Belarusian pavilion at the Soviet Exhibition of Achievements of the National Economy, a permanent trade show in Moscow.

After Yevsay had retired, Tanya Gamburg visited him. She saw the needs he had and offered to help around the house and wash his windows. He had been lonely since his wife passed away and needed some assistance, so he was glad for the help and company. However, he was puzzled by our team's care and asked Tanya why we cared about an old man like him.

Often survivors express similar feelings: "We understand people who take care of children and young people, but why do you give so much to take care of us elderly people?" Our answer is, "Yeshua called us to show His love and care to you. Therefore, we do so gladly."

Yevsay with Tanya and one of our volunteers, Steve

Tanya shared that her life was filled with joy from God, and she wanted to bring joy into others' lives as well. Yevsay was thankful for the friendship but told her he didn't need the fairytales from the Bible. He proudly proclaimed, "I am a scientifically minded atheist."

Their friendship continued to develop, but sadly, a year and a half later, Yevsay had a stroke and was bedridden. As he lay in bed day after day, he reflected on his upbringing, his atheistic indoctrination, and the possibility of the existence of God. He thought about what Tanya told him about God's love and eternal life, and he wanted to know more. He asked Tanya for Biblical literature and began to read and contemplate.

Due to his deteriorating health, his granddaughter came to visit him one day, expecting to say goodbye. She was surprised to find him sitting in the kitchen, drinking tea. Yevsay explained that his sudden recovery was nothing short of miraculous.

As he regained his strength, he took a greater interest in prayer, studying the Bible, and attending services at our congregation. He was overjoyed to find a loving spiritual family and at one service was thrilled to witness a Messianic Jewish wedding, an event that reminded him of his grandfather observing Shabbat. After a few years of studying and reflecting, he made another proclamation that was different from his position a few years earlier. "I was an atheist, an officer in the Soviet forces, but I've changed. Now I believe there is a God, and I believe in the Son of God, Yeshua."

Reflecting on his life, Yevsay said, "I am so thankful that God had mercy on an atheist like myself." He spent much of his life as an atheist and was glad he had come to believe in God. He had spent his career encouraging others not to believe in God, but the Lord had brought him to a place where he could embrace a belief in God and encourage others to do the same.

I (Chantal) remember the last time I saw Yevsay. It was in 2015, at a picnic our congregation organized. It had been a few months since I had seen him, and when I arrived, he greeted me with a strong hug, lifting my feet off the ground! I was impressed by the strength of my ninety-four-year-old friend. His excitement and joy were a result of sharing his life with his spiritual family whom he had come to love so much. He passed away a few months after this meeting, surrounded by the love of his family and his big spiritual family.

Yelena

Yelena's story is different. Since she had been adopted by Christians, she was raised in the church and could not imagine another expression of her faith. When she learned she was Jewish and later discovered our Messianic Jewish congregation, it was very meaningful for her. Coming from the Russian Orthodox church, the experience at our congregation was strange for her at first. As she learned about Jewish culture and traditions, she began to read the Bible with different eyes. Over time, she began to feel like she had returned home and came to love the atmosphere of our worship services. Seeing Jewish people living with faith in Jesus and seeing Him presented from a Jewish Biblical perspective opened her eyes to the Jewishness of her faith. Her Jewish identity began to grow, and she describes every meeting at Congregation Brit Chadasha as "a personal holiday."

Yelena with our team member, Anya, on the Sea of Galilee, Israel

A highlight of this journey to reconnect to her Jewish heritage and the Jewishness of her faith in Yeshua was when Yelena joined a group of eleven Belarusian Holocaust survivors on a ten-day excursion to Israel. Most of them had never been to their ancestral homeland. With God's help, we made their lifelong dreams come true by organizing this ten-day tour of the land. Yelena visited the wall honoring the Righteous Among the Nations at Yad Vashem where her adopted parents' names are inscribed. Helping her find their names was an emotional and meaningful moment.

When we first arrived in Belarus, we prayed that we would be able to help Holocaust survivors reconnect not only with their Jewishness but most importantly know the love of God. What we did not expect was that we would become like family to many of them.

One particularly moving example of this took place during a vacation retreat we organized for the survivors. We were talking with Yelena, Zoya, and Lydia, enjoying the cool evening breeze and our warm conversation with these precious ladies. They told us how they considered us family. We also felt like they were family and wondered if they saw us like siblings or maybe a son or daughter. They shocked us by saying, "You know, you are like a mom and dad to us." We were stunned to realize that people who were much older than us saw us in a parental role.

They explained that the Holocaust had made them all orphans, but they were experiencing parental love through the way that we cared for them, worried about them, and checked to see what we could do to make them comfortable and happy. It was humbling to hear these dear, grandmotherly ladies describe us this way. It was so moving to hear them explain what our care meant to them. These children of the Holocaust had been robbed of their childhood and their parents. Now as adults, they were being touched by the love of their heavenly Abba (Father) through the compassion and care we and our team showed them.

Sima and Chantal

Sima

Sima is another member of the National Association leadership group with whom we became like family. She always impressed us as a person who was interested in the spiritual aspect of life. It has been so gratifying to see that through her connection with our family and our team, her faith in God and conviction that Yeshua loves her keeps growing.

Through the time we spent with her, sitting in her apartment drinking tea and talking, we saw how her wounded heart was healing.

One event that was particularly meaningful and cathartic for her was when our oldest granddaughter, Eliana, and her family dedicated her bat mitzvah to Sima's sisters. Berta and Nechama were murdered by the Nazis before they reached the bat mitzvah age of twelve. Eliana planted two trees in Israel in honor of Sima's sisters. Sima told us, with tears in her eyes, that what Eliana did was one of the most meaningful and healing experiences of her life. To this day, she carries a certificate that states trees were planted in Israel in memory of her sisters and is always proud to show it to others. We can only say how grateful our family is to be able to bring comfort and blessing to dear people like Sima who suffered things that no human being should ever suffer.

Leonid

We are always glad to participate in bringing honor to the families of survivors, but in Leonid's case, we had an amazing opportunity to play a role in reuniting him with members of his family!

We became good friends with Leonid a few years before he passed away. He had suffered many health problems, had only one lung and one kidney, and survived a heart attack. He was a heavy smoker, yet he climbed four flights of stairs to his apartment each day since there was no elevator in his building. Having survived the Minsk Ghetto and four concentration camps, he was a strong-willed man who was motivated to tell his story so the world would never forget. He was determined to share what happened in the ghetto where he lost twenty-eight members of his family, some murdered before his eyes. Leonid wanted the world to know that he felt the ghettos should be called "death camps" so no one would mistakenly think of them as Jewish residential areas.

To achieve this goal, he gave speeches in Belarus and abroad. He wrote his memoir, *Such a Thing Must Not Be Forgotten,* a work he gave us permission to translate and publish in English. He even expressed his desire to accompany us to the United States to conduct speaking tours and tell people about Belarus's Holocaust experiences. To my (Stewart's) amazement, he told me, "I have two reasons for wanting to travel with you. The primary reason is to give people a firsthand account of what innocent Jewish people suffered in the ghettos and concentration camps. The second reason is also important to me. I want to tell people about how you, Chantal, and your team are doing such an important and holy work in Belarus for me and all the Holocaust survivors." We were deeply moved by these sincere words. Unfortunately, his health would not allow him to make this trip.

Like many survivors, his life after the war had been difficult. One thing he deeply regretted was being forced by the KGB to cut ties with relatives living in the United States.

After World War II ended, Leonid's aunt, who had moved to America before the war, learned of his survival and began sending him packages. The KGB learned of this and threatened him. They told him to stop embarrassing the Soviet Union by accepting her gifts and compelled him to write a letter to inform his aunt and her family that his country was able to care for him and he did not need their charity. The loss of contact with them was an added pain he had to bear.

In 2014, as I (Chantal) hosted a tour about Eastern European Jewry for Messianic Youth, we arranged for some of the youth to meet Leonid and hear his story. A young woman who led the group was touched when hearing how he lost contact with his relatives who lived in the States due to the Cold War. She felt she had been given the mission to find his relatives. Working with nothing but a name and a few photos, she miraculously found them after about six months of searching.

Soon after this, I organized a trip for Leonid's relatives to meet him in Minsk. As Stewart and I waited with him in the airport, I noticed how grim he looked and asked if he felt excited to finally meet his family. He gave me a surprised look and said, "No, Chantal, this is a sad day." I could feel his sorrow for the decades he had been prevented from corresponding with his relatives. So much time had been stolen from him! I empathized with him, but this was not the time for sorrow. I said, "Leonid, the fact that you are meeting them, even after all these years, should make it a joyful day. It's a day to celebrate!" He turned and looked at me with his stern, blue eyes, and although I had come to know him well, I was unsure what was going through his mind.

After having dinner with his family that evening, he gave a short speech that began, "Indeed today is a joyful day." Beneath that hardened exterior, he was a deeply wounded man with a very tender heart.

*Leonid with Chantal and her granddaughter, Elianna
picking mushrooms in the forest*

Once while I (Stewart) was having a pleasant visit with Leonid in his apartment, accompanied by two members of our team, Vika and Tanya, the topic of spirituality came up. We were discussing the theme of his book, *Such a Thing Must Not Be Forgotten,* and his concern that the Holocaust must never be forgotten. As the conversation continued, I shared with Leonid that I believed God would also like us to never forget some things. I believed He hopes we will never forget that He gives us all things to sustain our life as well as all the beauty of nature, all of this and more, because He is good and loves us.

Leonid got angry. "Stewart, how can you tell me God is good when the Nazis came to torture and murder Jews while wearing the words Gott Mit Uns (God with us) on their belt buckles and did such horrible things to us in the name of Jesus?"

I reflected for a moment, feeling that this was an important moment in our relationship and his relationship with God. I said, "Leonid, what if I told you I was President Vladimir Putin or President George Bush? You would call me a liar, because you know I do not resemble them in any way. Likewise, the Nazis do not resemble Messiah Yeshua in their behavior. When they claimed God was with them, they were liars. If you want a better picture of what Yeshua represents, take a look at Vika and Tanya. They are motivated to love and serve others because of their relationship with the one who claims to be the Messiah of Israel, the savior of the world, Yeshua."

Leonid had known Vika and Tanya for many years and felt they were two of the kindest and most goodhearted people he had ever met. I perceived his heart and mind were opening to the possibility that God was good and in fact loved him.

Soon after this, he asked Tanya for a copy of a booklet I wrote with the elders of Congregation Brit Chadasha entitled "First Steps with the Messiah of Israel." We wrote this booklet especially for the survivors to help them understand God's plan of redemption for mankind through Messiah Yeshua.

We spent many tender moments with him in the last months of his life before he passed away in October 2015 at the age of eighty-eight. We cherish the memories of those times to this day.

It always brings us so much joy when, by God's grace and with the help of our team, we can bring comfort, a renewed interest in God, and healing to the emotional scars survivors carried from the Holocaust.

Lydia with our team member, Olya,
during the holiday of Purim

Lydia

Lydia connected with us after receiving a holiday food package. One of our initiatives is to help survivors celebrate Jewish holidays by providing them the food they need to prepare a holiday meal. Soon after receiving her package, Lydia began attending our Shabbat services. She felt loved and accepted there. The more she attended, the more Lydia felt that she belonged. After being orphaned in the Holocaust, she had now been adopted into the family of God through her newfound faith in Yeshua. The members of the congregation became her mishpocha (family).

Though she was still haunted by feelings of fear and horror from the trauma of her childhood, she found a good measure of healing in knowing that her Heavenly Father cared for and loved her, as did her good friends on our team. One day, she shared with us how she realized that "healing comes from God to our wounded hearts. We feel God's care for us, and we are learning more about our God who helps us in everything."

Lova and Raisa with Stewart

Lova

The Holocaust left Lova Kravets with nothing but emotional scars. Having been separated from his sister in the orphanage, he felt like he had no one. After he was old enough to leave the orphanage, he reconnected with his sister, served in the army, and then got a job as a factory worker.

His loneliness began to dissipate when he met and married Raisa and had two daughters, Liza and Natasha. Late in life, he witnessed his daughters and their children becoming believers in Yeshua. However, this did not interest him, since he felt it was not for the Jewish people. Lova was also part of the National Association of Holocaust Survivors leadership team. As a result of the time we spent with him, our relationship began to grow. He told us how our help and love encouraged him and made him feel supported. This support and love was especially important during his final years as he battled cancer.

As the years passed, we discovered that he was observing the lives of followers of Yeshua. He attended our monthly meetings with the leadership of the National Association of Holocaust Survivors. At the meetings, he listened carefully when the discussions turned to God and how Yeshua fulfilled the prophecies of the Jewish prophets recorded in Tanakh. He was skeptical for a long time, but he was more open to my (Stewart) perspective because I was Jewish, not a gentile, and I spoke of Yeshua as one of our own—a Jew who lived in Israel.

After many years of diligent study and contemplation, Lova concluded that a Jewish person could believe in Yeshua after all, especially since many thousands of Jewish people who had lived in Yeshua's time had believed in Him. It also encouraged him to discover that there are many Jewish people today who believe in Yeshua and maintain their Jewish identity.

The last time we saw him, we were greeted by a scene we will never forget. As we entered his apartment, the usually reserved Lova greeted us warmly, raised his arms, and began thanking God for all He had done in his life and for sending Yeshua. It was so moving to witness his joyful proclamation. It turned out that he had been reading the Bible and some books about his newfound faith in Yeshua, and he was excited to tell us what he had discovered. Lova continued to read the Bible with a desire to discover new things and grow closer to God until he went to be with his Lord in January 2018 at the age of eighty-seven.

When we began our work, we were seeing so many lives touched that we quickly realized we could not do it alone. As we already mentioned, we built a team with members of our congregation who shared our heart to serve and bring Yeshua's love and comfort to the Holocaust survivors. The survivors in turn were very appreciative and many developed deep relationships with members of our team. With devotion, compassion, and self-sacrifice, our team has been instrumental in ministering to the practical, emotional, and spiritual needs of many more survivors than we would have been able to on our own. They play a key role in many of the following stories.

Irina (right) with her sister, Alla (left), and Tanya

Irina

Irina was another survivor whose life was profoundly touched by Tanya Gamburg. They met when Tanya brought her a gift basket for the holidays. Soon Tanya began helping her with shopping and practical needs around her apartment. Like Yevsay and many others, Irina was curious to know what motivated Tanya and others from our team to do all this. After hearing about God's love and Messiah Yeshua's suffering, she felt that God could understand her suffering.

This began her pursuit of God. She said this:

"The love I felt when Tanya spoke and prayed for me was unlike anything I had ever felt before. For three years, I listened to the stories of Yeshua and welcomed people into my life from Stewart and Chantal's congregation in Minsk. In 2015, I made a firm decision that indeed Yeshua suffered and died for me and for all people because he loved us. He too had endured great pain. He understood the pain and evil of the world, and He chose to allow himself to experience it. It was a great gift to know that He hadn't abandoned me, but He was always trying to reach me. He found me and gave me a new beginning."

Irina with our team member, Valodya

When Irina was diagnosed with breast cancer, Tanya and our team supported and prayed for her. Irina was convinced that she would be fine in the hands of God and had no doubt that she would be rescued from her sickness. For various reasons, her surgery was delayed for almost a year. The doctors were shocked to find that during this time, the tumor had shrunk to almost nothing. She had experienced a miraculous healing! Soon after this, she decided to begin going with Tanya to visit and help other survivors, saying, "Once again God has given me the gift of life, and I am going to use it to help others."

Irina preparing a meal for Nella, another Holocaust survivor

Raisa

In many ways, Raisa's story is similar to Irina's. She had always been a spiritual seeker and was excited to discover our Bible studies being held in homes throughout Minsk. She became convinced of what the Tanakh and Brit Chadasha taught about the Jewish Messiah and decided that Yeshua was the Messiah of Israel.

Her faith was significantly strengthened when she experienced physical healing one night. She was suffering from swelling in her legs and could not walk. She explained how she woke up at 3:00 a.m. and began praying and touching her legs. She felt filled with joy and lightness and looked at her legs. They were healed. She was able to walk! Yeshua had supernaturally healed her!

Raisa was close to Tanya, and they often prayed together. One particularly memorable time they spent together was when Raisa's flat was being renovated. Tanya came to help her prepare a Shabbat meal, and they shared a joyful Shabbat by candlelight since there was no power.

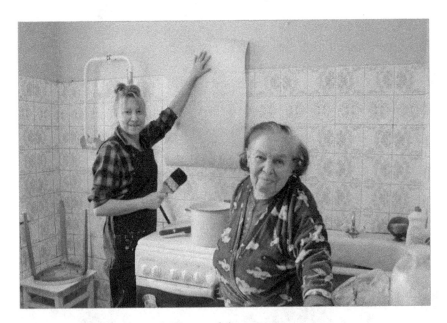

Tanya assisting Raisa with her apartment renovations

Rasia with our team members Trevor, Dalene, and Tanya

Raisa passed away in March 2017. Our team continues to help her sister, Vera, maintain Raisa's apartment, which is a special place to her as it brings back warm memories of her sister.

Lev (wearing his medals) with Stewart, Chantal, and their granddaughter, Eliana, at his one hundredth birthday celebration

Lev

Lev was also struggling with physical difficulties when we met him. He had passed out in the street and woke up in the hospital with a diagnosis that he would never walk again. Like many of the survivors, he was a fighter, and he fought to get out of bed and walk. He succeeded, and the day he was able to walk with a cane, he declared it was like being reborn and similar to how he felt when he had escaped the POW camp.

Lev with our team member, Dima, reading a booklet written by Stewart and the elders of Congregation Brit Chadasha about the Messiah of Israel

Lev appreciated the regular visits from our team. Dima, another member of our team, became like an adopted son to him. Dima gave him haircuts, helped him shave, ran errands, and spent time with him being a friend and a comfort. Lev's interest in spiritual things was piqued as he experienced the kindness and generosity that Dima and our team consistently demonstrated to him and his wife, Nina, while wanting nothing in return. At the age of ninety-four, he began examining Yeshua's claims in the Bible. After careful study, he became convinced that life does not end when we physically die and that Yeshua would usher him into eternity.

At first, Nina was reserved and skeptical, with no interest in the spiritual conversations Lev had with Dima, but with gentle nudging from Lev, Nina became more interested in the discussions. She was thankful for the help she received from Dima during her long, difficult battle with cancer, and because of the unconditional love she and Lev were shown, Nina became more and more interested in discussing spiritual questions.

After some time, she became bedridden due to her battle with cancer, so members of our team sometimes spent the night assisting her. One evening, Valya, another member of our team, described sensing God's presence in the room. She noticed Lev and Nina speaking to each other in a special and tender way, remembering many moments of their lives and asking forgiveness for times they may have hurt each other. After their conversation, Nina joyfully declared that she now understood that Yeshua was who He claimed to be.

The next day, she passed away peacefully. Lev grieved the loss of his beloved but at the same time stated that he had confidence that Yeshua provided life that did not end at physical death but continued into eternity. The thought that he would be reunited with Nina was of great comfort to him. In another tender moment, Lev shared with us that he was thankful that through his friendship with us, he learned about heaven where he believed he would be reunited with his wife and his friends. He passed away in August 2020 at the age of 102 and was ushered into that eternity to which he was looking forward.

Anatoly

Anatoly often helped sort the humanitarian aid that we brought into the country. After sorting the food, clothing, and personal care items, we would distribute these items to the 350 Holocaust survivors who lived in Minsk. Through his involvement, he got to work with me (Chantal) and shared how he had always believed that "someone" had helped and protected him throughout his life. This fundamental belief in God made him deeply appreciative that we always prayed before beginning to unload containers of aid.

Anatoly was very glad when our team members proposed to drive him to Shabbat service. He loved the Jewish atmosphere, the warm welcome, and acceptance he felt. He would look forward to this special day each week. Although he did not open his heart fully to the message of Yeshua at this time, many seeds were planted.

As the years passed, his wife, Maria's health deteriorated to the point that she was bedridden and needed continual care. Anatoly was her primary caregiver, which prevented him from attending the Shabbat service he so loved.

Anya, one of our team members began to visit them more regularly to offer the practical assistance as well as emotional and spiritual support they needed. Maria enjoyed praying with Anya, and through their time together, she let go of unforgiveness in her heart and accepted Yeshua's forgiveness. She began more enthusiastically reading the Bible and discussing what she learned with Anya. Gradually, Anatoly also took a more serious interest in the Bible. Since he could not read any longer due to his failing eyesight, he would have Maria and Anya read to him. Eventually, Anatoly opened his heart fully to the "someone" who had always been there for him, Messiah Yeshua.

Anatoly with his wife, Maria, and our team member, Yulia

Their next few years were defined by growing in their faith and joyful times fellowshipping with our team. Maria passed away in 2017, and a month later, at the age of eighty-eight, Anatoly joined her in eternity.

Alexander

We met Alexander Mysov when he traveled to Minsk to play music for other Holocaust survivors. Two of his daughters, Tamara and Larissa, and his grand-daughter, Yulia, all became followers of Yeshua at some of our first Shabbat services held in Minsk. When they attempted to share their new beliefs with him, his witty reply was that he believed in God "but not His relatives," referring to their belief that Yeshua was the Son of God.

Over the years, he watched his daughters' and granddaughters' lives improving as they became more caring, patient, and kind. Seeing how satisfied they were with life and the peace they found from their faith, he told Tamara that because God had not only allowed him to survive but had given him children who served God, he needed to come to Him. He asked her to do *t'vilah* (immerse him in water) as confirmation of his newfound faith in the Son of God. He wanted to be immersed because he wanted to follow the example of the first-century Jewish followers of Yeshua. Just after t'vilah, Tamara saw tears in his eyes. This profoundly impacted her since she had never seen him cry. She concluded that his wounded heart was being healed by the love of the God of Israel.

Alexander with his granddaughter, Yulia

Alexander passed on to be with the Lord on February 18, 2015, leaving his children, grandchildren, and great-grandchildren with many fond memories and a legacy of music. Tamara, Larisa, Yulia, and his great-grandsons, David, and Philip, all followed in his footsteps as musicians. David mastered the violin, his great-grandfather's favorite instrument to play before he was injured in the war.

Yulia and her husband, Valodya, have been part of our team since 1995. They have often played music at our events for Holocaust survivors and befriended many of them.

Vladimir

Yulia and Valodya became particularly close to Vladimir Sverdlov. All his life, Vladimir was motivated by his love and gratitude to Baba Alesya, the woman who had saved his life during the Holocaust. He sought to do nice things for Christians out of respect for her and her faith. He felt that Christians and Jews had similar values and that God's will was done through good people. Remembering Baba Alesya's admonitions to believe in God, he attended an Orthodox synagogue but did not feel welcomed or accepted because he could not pray in Hebrew. He visited a Russian Orthodox church but did not like the service and found the long periods of standing to be tiring. When he discovered our Messianic Jewish congregation, he enjoyed the service very much and felt like he had found a home for his Jewish soul.

Vladimir and his wife, Maria, with Yulia and J. L. Corey

He became part of the congregation and insisted on giving some of his small pension to our building fund to construct the first Messianic Jewish Synagogue/Ministry Center in Belarus. Vladimir stated, "As a Jew, I say that this building should be for many, many generations. Jews have always been here, and we are thankful for the construction of the first Messianic Jewish Synagogue of Belarus. Once it is built, people will come, and we will rejoice." Vladimir passed away on April 30, 2021 at the age of ninety-one.

Mikhail

When Mikhail Treister replaced Felix Lipsky as the leader of the National Association of Holocaust Survivors, our first impression was that he was a stern man. Despite his reserved nature, he became one of our dearest friends. We became so close that he gave us the privilege of publishing the English translation of his memoir, *Gleams of Memory,* which tells the story of his suffering at the hands of the Nazis and Communists.

Mikhail with Chantal and Stewart, with a copy of Mikhail's memoir
Gleams of Memory, *which they published in English*

Through the events and gatherings that we organized for the survivors, we began to see another side of Mikhail. During one Chanukah party, we decided to play dreidel, the traditional game associated with the holiday. We were surprised that most of the survivors had never played before, and we recognized this was yet another example of their childhoods that had been destroyed by the Nazis. We were delighted to see their faces light up as they began laughing and teasing each other. Even Mikhail couldn't hide his excitement.

While other survivors often took a more active interest in our beliefs, Mikhail frequently said, "I love you and your team. I envy your faith, but my experiences in the Holocaust and under the Soviets make it difficult for me to go there (to consider the existence of a good God)." We understood his struggles. His unemotional, determined nature meant that he was firm in his scientific, atheistic beliefs.

Later in life, as he faced a battle with cancer, Mikhail developed a greater interest in spiritual matters. As he thought about his life, he remembered an accident he had while climbing a mountain years before. He had fallen and injured one of his limbs and was bleeding heavily. His hiking companions realized that he would bleed to death if the wound was not stitched closed, but they had no medical equipment and had not seen anyone else on the trail all day. Out of nowhere, a man appeared on the trail. He turned out to be a doctor who happened to have surgical equipment with him, and he saved Mikhail's life by treating his wound. As he thought back to this event, Mikhail wondered if it was possible that God existed and was watching out for him that day and at other times in his life.

As Mikhail continued to battle cancer, Roman (a leader in our Messianic Congregation in Minsk) and I (Stewart) drove him to a specialist for treatment. On the way, I asked if he had ever read the Brit Chadasha (New Testament), and he said that he had, many years before. He added that if we could give him something short to read, he would do it. I was leaving the country the next day, so I asked Roman to give him a booklet.

Shortly after receiving it, Mikhail asked Roman to visit him again. When he arrived, Mikhail (with his usual wit) asked, "How do I join your club?"

Roman was confused, and Mikhail clarified with a simple, yet powerful statement. "I believe as you do, and I want you to pray for me." Roman and Mikhail discussed further, and after Roman was convinced that Mikhail understood what faith in Yeshua was all about, they prayed together, and Mikhail gave his life to Yeshua. It is interesting to note that Mikhail recounted in his memoir that he had long envied people who had strong beliefs, and he had now experienced such a belief himself.

We spent twelve years living in Minsk and continue to spend a few months every year visiting survivors and encouraging our team in Belarus. We planned one of our visits to coincide with Mikhail's ninetieth birthday. He was weak and could barely speak, but we had a special and moving time with him. When the time came to leave his apartment, it was incredibly difficult to say goodbye! We took his hand into our hands and prayed for him. Despite his weakened state, we were so moved by the feeling of love and friendship as he held our hands tightly and with a unique warmth.

Two days after this visit, our dear friend Mikhail went to be with the Lord. Although we miss him greatly, we know one day we will meet again.

Developing these special friendships with so many Holocaust survivors is something we consider to be one of the greatest privileges of our lives. These dear people who have survived so much suffering and hate have such great wisdom, strength, and courage. Our lives have been enriched by knowing and serving them. It is such a joy for us to help them connect with their Jewish identity, provide practical everyday help, and see God work in their lives as we travel with them on their spiritual journeys.

Although God has blessed our work in amazing ways, and we rejoice knowing that so many survivors have been deeply touched by the life-transforming love of God, it has nevertheless been very difficult for us to deal with the evil and horrifying suffering our friends have experienced and shared with us.

I (Stewart) remember that when we were preparing to move to Belarus, my mind turned toward the reality that we would face people who survived some of the worst horrors in human history. Having watched the film *Schindler's List*, which had recently been released, and seeing the graphic and gut-wrenching depictions of the Holocaust, I was deeply troubled. Knowing that Belarus had been devastated by the Holocaust, I found myself asking God, "How can I talk about Your love for my Jewish people with those who had endured so much suffering?"

A group of Holocaust survivors from Belarus, including Zoya, Sima, Lydia, and Yelena, during a trip Stewart and Chantal organized to the Jewish homeland, Israel

It was an inner crisis. After struggling with this question for some time, I was reconfirmed in my heart that although I could not understand everything about life or God's interactions with the tragedy, evil, and injustice in human history (who can?), I could move forward with what I did know. Based on what Scripture says and my personal experiences since following the path of love and sacrificial service that Messiah Yeshua modeled, I felt reassured that God indeed is good and loving. He is the God of healing and redemption.

Over the past twenty-six years, many of our friends among the Holocaust survivors have asked similar questions. "Does God really exist? How could He allow the Holocaust? Is God good?" No matter how many times we are face to face with a survivor who asks these questions, the gravity and deep pain behind them impacts us and evokes deep compassion that we can only explain as God's love in our hearts for our friends. I readily admit that I cannot give a complete answer, and I don't think anyone can fully answer such questions.

When Holocaust survivors ask such hard questions, it is often evident that they have a deep desire, despite everything they have endured, to believe that there is a God and that He indeed is good.

I begin by explaining what the Bible teaches about the good and loving nature of God and how He desires for all people to relate to one another in love. In the Tanakh and Brit Chadasha, God instructs people to love our neighbor as we love ourselves and to treat others like we would like to be treated. I go on to say that God also gave mankind free will, and sadly, many people use that freedom to do evil and ignore God's commands and instructions. I share with them how people who are overcome with evil and hate chose to rebel against God and His ways, and it was their evil choices that created the Holocaust. Because we have been given the freedom by our Creator to choose between good and evil. Some of us choose to be gracious, loving, and kind while, tragically, others choose unimaginable evils like those of the Holocaust.

"See, I have set before you today life and good, and death and evil. Therefore, choose life" (Deuteronomy 30:15, 19b).[21]

I also find it helps the survivors when I share insight I gained from these amazing and revealing words that Yeshua spoke and are recorded in the book of Matthew:

> Then the King will say to those on His right, "Come, you who are blessed by My Father, inherit the kingdom prepared for you from the foundation of the world. For I was hungry, and you gave Me something to eat; I was thirsty and you gave Me something to drink; I was a stranger and you invited Me in; I was naked and you clothed Me; I was sick and you visited Me; I was in prison and you came to Me." Then the righteous will answer Him, "Lord,

when did we see You hungry and feed You? Or thirsty and give You something to drink? And when did we see You a stranger and invite You in? Or naked and clothe You? When did we see You sick, or in prison, and come to You?" And answering, the King will say to them, "Amen, I tell you, whatever you did to one of the least of these My brethren, you did it to Me" (Matthew 25:34–40).[22]

This passage in Matthew reveals that whenever we do good to others, we are also doing good to Messiah. The opposite is also true; whenever we withhold good from others or do evil to others, we are doing evil or withholding good from the Messiah as well. We can also conclude from this passage of Scripture that when we suffer evil, Yeshua shares in our sufferings.

Another passage that is enlightening to survivors who ask these questions about God is written by the Jewish prophet Isaiah about seven hundred years before Yeshua was born.

"Surely He has borne our griefs and carried our sorrows; yet we esteemed Him stricken, smitten by God and afflicted. But He was wounded for our transgressions, He was bruised for our iniquities; the chastisement for our peace was upon Him, and by His stripes, we are healed." (Isaiah 53:4–5)[23]

Putting it all together with these prophetic words recorded in the book of Isaiah, I share that God's love for all people motivated Him to give us Messiah Yeshua to suffer with us and for us. He gave His life as an atonement for our sins so that we can be in fellowship with God forever.

Over the years, we have looked into many pain-filled and questioning eyes as we attempt to bring comfort and provide some answers to our friends who have experienced so much evil. With all the compassion the Lord enables us to have, we usually conclude our response with words like these: "We believe Messiah Yeshua wants you to know that He was with you when you suffered in the Holocaust. He is with you now, and because He loves you so much, He wants to be with you and all of us forever in eternity."

Chantal and I are humbled when we see from the look on their faces and the words they share after such conversations that the Spirit of God is bringing some comfort to their souls and a greater understanding of the workings of God in the midst of suffering and evil.

It is our heartfelt prayer and desire that while they are still with us, many more Holocaust survivors would find the deep inner healing and heavenly comfort that can come only through knowing and experiencing Yeshua's love.

As you can imagine, many survivors struggle with faith and the difficult questions surrounding the goodness of God. Elie Wiesel describes Auschwitz as a place where the Nazis murdered his faith.

"Never shall I forget that night, the first night in camp, which had turned my life into one long night...never shall I forget that smoke. Never shall I forget the little faces of the children, whose bodies I saw turned into wreaths of smoke beneath a silent blue sky. Never shall I forget those flames which consumed my faith forever... Never shall I forget those moments which murdered my God."[24]

The horrors of the Holocaust "murdered" many survivors' faith in God and mankind. Yet, we have seen that even in the depth of sorrow and horrific suffering, the unconditional love of God can penetrate through this unthinkable pain and reach the hearts of those He loves so dearly to bring hope, healing, and redemption. God uses ordinary people who are willing to say "yes" to bring His perfect love to comfort His people and to show Holocaust survivors in simple and practical ways that they are loved and were never forgotten.

The people you have met in the pages of this book are incredibly strong to have survived so much horror, yet they are some of the warmest people one could ever meet. Many maintain a positive attitude despite everything they suffered. They are amazing people, and it has long been our desire to share their stories. As we have sought to serve them, they have tremendously enriched our lives. It is one of our life's greatest gifts to share in their spiritual journeys and see survivors find new faith, joy, and eternal life through the lover of their souls, Messiah Yeshua.

We are honored to have been able to share their stories with you.

Addendum:
Responding to Modern-Day Antisemitism and Evil

———

WE UNDERSTAND THAT THESE STORIES OF MAN'S CRUELTY TO HIS fellow man and the suffering of innocent Jewish children, men, and women have been difficult to read. There may have been times when you were brought to tears at the stories of overwhelming tragedy, suffering, and loss. You may have felt anger or horror to hear of the brutal and merciless ways that the Jewish people and other victims of the Nazis were treated.

For many survivors, retelling these stories is difficult. Reliving the trauma of their youth was not easy, but they did it so that the world will know the facts and to honor the memory of their loved ones, rescuers, and the six million innocent Jewish people who perished.

What can be gained by reliving and remembering stories filled with such trauma and tragedy? How should we respond to accounts of such evil and hate?

There are three ways. The first was mentioned in the last chapter. We can ask questions. We can struggle to understand why and how such things could occur. Such a response is justified and understandable.

The distinguished rabbi and philosopher Joseph Soloveitchik (a Belarusian Jew who immigrated to the United States a few years before the Nazis invaded his country) wrote of two ways that we can respond to the Holocaust and any other evil that we face.

We can react passively, which means we only ask questions like "Why did this happen?"

We can react actively and ask questions like "Since this has happened, how should I act? What can I do?"[25]

Rabbi Soloveitchik felt that the second response was a more profitable route. Asking hard questions about the Holocaust is justifiable, but the survivors shared their stories so we can learn from them.

Some wrote books, and others served as leaders of the National Association of Holocaust Survivors, caring for their fellow survivors. We left the comforts of the United States to serve them and wrote this book to help share and preserve their stories.

Now that you have heard these stories, you can choose how to respond. How will you act?

The greatest way one can act is to resolve to never allow ourselves to be indifferent to evil and suffering! Indifference is the third choice when faced with evil such as the Holocaust. If only more people had refused indifference during the dark days of the Holocaust, who knows what could have happened.

World-renowned survivor and author Elie Wiesel said it this way: "I swore never to be silent whenever and wherever human beings endure suffering and humiliation. Silence encourages the tormentor, never the tormented."

Today we see antisemitism rising again around the world. We see attacks on Jewish communities and individuals increasing. We see unfair and false accusations leveled against Israel, the only Jewish state in the world. We see other minority groups demonized, threatened, and attacked, and we see despicable efforts to deny that the horrors of the Holocaust even happened!

Our friends told their stories with the hope that such things will never happen again. Their experiences remind us of the danger of being silent and indifferent to evil.

First, they came for the communists, and I did not speak because
I was not a communist.
Then, they came for the trade unionists, and I did not speak
because I was not a trade unionist.
Then, they came for the Jews, and I did not speak because I was
not a Jew.
Then they came for me, and there was no one left to speak.

—PASTOR MARTIN NIEMÖLLER

These words were written by a German pastor who had supported Hitler during his rise to power. Only after the Nazis were in full control did he begin to oppose their religious agenda. He did so because it began to impact him personally. However, at that point, he showed no concern for the Jewish people and others who were suffering cruel persecution at the hands of the Nazis. Soon, he found himself a political prisoner in the Dachau concentration camp, alongside Jews, Communists, and many others whose suffering he had been indifferent toward.

The writer of the book of Hebrews in the Brit Chadasha encouraged us to "let brotherly love continue...Remember the prisoners as if you were fellow prisoners and those who are mistreated as if you also were suffering bodily." (Hebrews 13:1, 3)[26]

Yeshua, the Messiah of Israel, also known in the Scriptures as the King of Kings, made clear God's commands relating to man's relationship to his fellow man. "You shall love your neighbor as yourself...do to others what you would want them to do to you—for this is the Torah and the Prophets" (Matthew 22:39, 7:12).[27] We trust that you will agree that His words are as important for us today as they have ever been.

We hope that our friends' stories will motivate you to never be indifferent, to always stand for justice. Stories like these force each of us to examine our lives and ask ourselves some questions. What would God require of me if I were to face similar circumstances? What would I do? Would I obey Him and do the right thing, or would I ignore my responsibility to God and my fellow man? Let us stand against antisemitism and all forms of prejudice, racism, and bigotry to fulfill the hope that such horrors will never again be allowed. When faced with evil, let us choose to act with prayerful hearts and hold high the banners of God's love, truth, and justice.

As the oft-quoted and insightful maxim warns, "For evil to flourish, it only requires good men to do nothing." Never again!

Glossary

Aktion (pl. Aktionen): German for "action," used to refer to a planned act of violence against the Jewish people. Russian speakers refer to these events as pogroms.

Aliyah (עליה): Hebrew for the act of going up or ascending. Literally, the term refers to ascending to Jerusalem, which sits at a higher elevation than the surrounding region of Israel. It is used to describe the act of Jewish emigration and return to the Jewish homeland.

Ashkenazi (Ashkenazim): The cultural identity of European Jewry found from Germany to Russia.

Brit Chadasha: Hebrew for "new covenant." It refers to the New Testament. In this book, it is also the name of the Messianic congregation the Winograds established in Minsk.

Chernobyl: The location of a Soviet nuclear power plant in northern Ukraine (south of the border of Belarus). On April 26, 1986, the reactor exploded, causing the largest nuclear disaster in history.

Einsatzgruppe (pl. Einsatzgruppen): German for "task force." Refers to the killing squads that followed the German army during the invasion of the Soviet Union.

Gaswagen/Dushegubka (Душегубка): German for "gas vehicle" ("soul killer" in Russian). Vans with airtight cargo compartment designed kill the occupants by asphyxiation with carbon monoxide from the engine.

Judenrat: German for "Jewish Council." A Nazi-created institution of prominent Jewish community figures given the responsibility of overseeing the administration of daily life for the Jewish population.

Judenrein: German for "cleansed of Jews." Judenfrei (free of Jews) is an equivalent term. Used by the Nazis to describe areas where all Jewish residents had been deported or murdered.

KGB (КГБ): The Soviet "Committee for State Security," which operated intelligence services and the secret police.

Malina (малина): Russian for "raspberry." A slang term to describe a hiding place for people. Used by the prisoners in the ghetto to describe the places they constructed to hide from the Nazis.

Nazi: Acronym for the Nationalsozialistische Deutsche Arbeiterpartei (National Socialist German Workers Party). In this book, the term Nazi, rather than German, is used to focus on the fact that these individuals shared or supported the ideological theories of racial superiority and antisemitism that were foundational to the Nazi Party. Not all Nazis were Germans (many including Hitler were Austrians). The Russian-speaking world uses the term "Fascist" instead of Nazi.

Pogrom: A violent or mob action with the approval of the governing authorities. Used in reference to events during the Russian Empire era and the Nazi Aktion.

Polizei: German for "police." The term describes local populations including Ukrainians, Belarusians, Poles, Lithuanians, etc. who volunteered or were forced to work as police forces for the Nazis. They often guarded the ghettos and concentration camps and participated in many of the pogroms and acts of mass murder.

Refusenik: Jewish individuals who were denied permission to make aliyah or emigrate to Israel from the Soviet Union.

Shoah (שואה): Hebrew word for the Holocaust that means total devastation. Holocaust and Shoah are used interchangeably in this book.

Shtetl: A small predominantly Jewish village in Eastern Europe.

SMERSH (СМЕРШ): An acronym that means "Death to Spies." It refers to the Soviet organization that oversaw counterintelligence agencies and sought to protect the Soviet Union from spies during the war.

Slavic: The predominant shared ethno-linguistic identity found in Eastern Europe. Includes Russians, Belarusians, Ukrainians, and various Balkan nations.

Sonderkommando: German for "special unit." Used to refer to Jewish prisoners who were forced to work in death camps, removing and disposing of the bodies of their fellow Jews.

Tanakh (תנ״ך): An acronym describing the Jewish Bible (the Christian Old Testament).

Union of Soviet Socialist Republics: The Soviet Union or USSR was the Communist country that consisted of a union of smaller states (Russia, Belarus, Ukraine, Kazakhstan, and others). The USSR was formed in 1922 after the Communist Russian Revolution, and it collapsed in 1991.

Vernichtungslager: German for "extermination camp." Used to refer to the Polish camps of Treblinka, Sobibor, Belzec, and Chelmno and the Belarusian location of Maly Trostenets. It can also describe the Majdanek and Auschwitz-Birkenau hybrid locations where extermination functions took place as part of a larger concentration camp complex.

Wehrmacht: The armed forces of Nazi Germany. Including the Army, Navy, and Luftwaffe (Air Force). The SS and Einsatzgruppen were not part of the Wehrmacht but were a separate paramilitary organization under the command of Heinrich Himmler.

Yad Vashem (יד ושם): The National Holocaust Museum, memorial, and research center of Israel. It is dedicated to preserving the memory and names of each victim of the Shoah as well as recognizing the Righteous Among the Nations who assisted the Jewish people during the Shoah.

Yeshua: The Hebrew version of the name Jesus.

Bibliography

⸙

Bajohr, Frank, and Andrea Löw, eds. *The Holocaust and European Societies: Social Processes and Social Dynamics.* London: Macmillan, 2016.

"Belarus," European Jewish Congress, https://eurojewcong.org/communities/belarus.

"Belarus," The YIVO Encyclopedia of Jews in Eastern Europe, YIVO Institute for Jewish Research, https://yivoencyclopedia.org/article.aspx/Belarus.

Bronstein, Hilda, and Bett Demby, eds. *We Remember Lest the World Forget.* Minsk: JewishGen, 2012.

Browning, Christopher. *Ordinary Men, Reserve Police Battalion 101 and the Final Solution in Poland.* New York: HarperCollins, 1992.

Хроника Минского гетто 1–3 *(Chronicle of the Minsk Ghetto 1–3).* Documentary. Режиссер Владимир Луцкий (Producer Vladimir Lutsky). Belarus, 2013.

Desbois, Fr. Patrick. *The Holocaust by Bullets.* New York: Palgrave MacMillan, 2008.

Epstein, Barbara. *The Minsk Ghetto 1941–1943: Jewish Resistance and Soviet Internationalism.* Berkley: University of California Press, 2008.

Goldberg, Jeffrey. "Ed Zwick on Passivity, Jewish Power, and Hamas." *The Atlantic,* January 16, 2009.

Hjelmgaard, Kim. "In Secretive Belarus, Chernobyl's Impact Is Breathtakingly Grim." *USA TODAY,* April 18, 2016.

The Holy Bible (New International Version). Grand Rapids: Zondervan, 1978.

The Holy Bible (Tree of Life Version). Messianic Jewish Family Bible Society. Grand Rapids: Baker, 2015.

Kershner, Isabel. "Pardon Plea by Adolf Eichmann, Nazi War Criminal, Is Made Public." *New York Times,* January 27, 2016.

Paldiel, Mordecai. *Saving One's Own: Jewish Rescuers during the Holocaust.* Lincoln: University of Nebraska Press, 2017.

"Rettendes Brot, Außergenwöhnliche Überlebensgeschichten in der Kriegzeit," Horst Krüger, International Christian Embassy Jerusalem, May 23, 2013, https://de.icej.org/news/special-reports/rettendes-brot.

Office of United States Chief of Counsel for Prosecution of Axis Criminality. *Nazi Conspiracy and Aggression: Volume III.* Washington, DC: US Government Printing Office, 1946.

"Suicide rate in 1990 vs 2017," Our World in Data, https://ourworldindata.org.

Rubenstein, Leonid. "Such a Thing Must Not Be Forgotten." Unpublished manuscript. Accessed 2021. Typescript.

Sacks, Jonathan. *Crisis and Covenant: Jewish Thought After the Holocaust.* Manchester: Manchester University Press, 1992.

Sanford, Teirre. "Memory of the Minsk Ghetto: The Interaction of Genre and Generations after the Holocaust." Doctoral diss., University of Virginia, 2020.

Smilovitsky, Leonid. "The Rechitsa Pogrom (October 1905)." Tel Aviv: 1997.

Treister, Michael. *Gleams of Memory.* Minsk: Noah's Ark, 2013.

Wiesel, Elie. *Night.* New York: Penguin, 2006.

Yad Vashem. Righteous Among the Nations Database. https://righteous.yadvashem.org/?/search.html?language=en

Yahad-In Unum, https://www.yahadinunum.org.

Notes

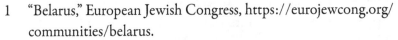

1   "Belarus," European Jewish Congress, https://eurojewcong.org/communities/belarus.

2   Leonid Smilovitsky, "The Rechitsa Pogrom (October 1905)" (Tel Aviv: 1997).

3   "Belarus," The YIVO Encyclopedia of Jews in Eastern Europe, YIVO Institute for Jewish Research, https://yivoencyclopedia.org/article.aspx/Belarus.

4   The Holy Bible (New International Version). (Grand Rapids: Zondervan, 1978).

5   Fr. Patrick Desbois, The Holocaust by Bullets (New York: Palgrave MacMillan, 2008).

6   "The Final Solution: Göring Commission to Heydrich." Dawidowicz, Lucy S. A Holocaust Reader. (West Orange: Behrman, 1976), 72–73.

7   Frank Bajohr and Andrea Löw, eds., The Holocaust and European Societies: Social Processes and Social Dynamics (London: MacMillan, 2016).

8   Office of United States Chief of Counsel for Prosecution of Axis Criminality, Nazi Conspiracy and Aggression: Volume III (Washington, DC: US Government Printing Office. 1946), 783–89.

9   Teirre Sanford, "Memory of the Minsk Ghetto: The Interaction of Genre and Generations after the Holocaust" (doctoral dissertation, University of Virginia, 2020), 95.

10 Isabel Kershner, "Pardon Plea by Adolf Eichmann, Nazi War Criminal, Is Made Public," *New York Times*, January 27, 2016.

11 Christopher Browning, *Ordinary Men, Reserve Police Battalion 101 and the Final Solution in Poland* (New York: HarperCollins, 1992).

12 Jeffrey Goldberg, "Ed Zwick on Passivity, Jewish Power, and Hamas," *The Atlantic*, January 16, 2009.

13 Mordecai Paldiel, Saving One's Own: Jewish Rescuers during the Holocaust (Lincoln: The Jewish Publication Society, 2017).

14 "Rettendes Brot, Außergenwöhnliche Überlebensgeschichten in der Kriegzeit," Horst Krüger, International Christian Embassy Jerusalem, May 23, 2013, https://de.icej.org/news/special-reports/rettendes-brot.

15 "PM Netanyahu at Dedication of Memorial for Righteous Among the Nations Diplomats at MFA." IsraeliPM, YouTube. February 5, 2018.

16 The Holy Bible (Tree of Life Version). Messianic Jewish Family Bible Society, (Grand Rapids: Baker, 2015).

17 Kim Hjelmgaard, "In Secretive Belarus, Chernobyl's Impact Is Breathtakingly Grim," *USA TODAY*, April 18, 2016.

18 "Suicide rate in 1990 vs 2017," Our World in Data, https://ourworldindata.org.

19 NIV.

20 TLV.

21 TLV.

22 TLV.

23 NIV.

24 Night, Eile Wiesel, New York: Hill and Wang, 1958. XVIII.

25 Jonathan Sacks, Crisis and Covenant: Jewish Thought After the Holocaust (New York: Penguin, 2006), 34.

26 TLV.

27 TLV.

About the Authors

STEWART AND CHANTAL WINOGRAD were married in August 1979. They have four wonderful children and eleven beloved grandchildren.

Stewart grew up in New York City. He was raised in a secular Ashkenazi Jewish family with ancestral roots across Europe, including Austria, the Bukovina region of Romania, and Belarus. In his late teens, he developed a desire to discover the purpose of life. At the age of 25, he found his answer in a place he never expected to... the Bible and the resurrection power of Jesus (Yeshua), the promised Messiah of Israel.

Chantal was raised in a non-Jewish secular family in Montreal, Canada. She was introduced to the concept of a personal relationship with Yeshua when she met Stewart in 1979. Through her relationship with Him, Yeshua gave her a great love and appreciation for the Jewish people and a heart like the Biblical character Ruth. The Jewish people have become her people just as the God of Israel (who is God of all) had become her God.

Stewart and Chantal moved to Belarus with their four children in response to what they believe was a calling and commission from God to restore Biblical spirituality to the Jewish people and all in Belarus. They lived in Belarus from 1995–2007 and through them, God birthed four Messianic Jewish Congregations, the Comfort for Holocaust Survivors Initiative you read about in the book, a Compassion for Orphans initiative, Camp Chalutzim for children and teens, and more. As of the date of the writing of this book they continue to oversee the work in Belarus and visit the country regularly.

Stewart is an ordained Messianic Jewish Rabbi. He and Chantal are co-founders of Reach Initiative International, a Messianic Jewish ministry serving in Israel, Belarus, India, and North America.

To learn more about Reach Initiative International or to contact Stewart and Chantal please visit reachii.org.

J. L. COREY's passion for history has led him to travel the globe, spending significant amounts of time living in Europe and the Middle East.

A native of upstate New York, he holds degrees in Biblical studies (Calvary Chapel Bible College, 2016), history (Liberty University, 2018), and Jewish studies (The Hebrew University of Jerusalem, 2021).

His areas of interest and expertise include German history, connections and correlations between religion and violence, and how the memory of the Holocaust and other acts of genocide and atrocities impact culture.

J. L.'s work has recently been featured in an online public history exhibition, In Between Jerusalem and Munich, produced in partnership between the Ludwig Maximillian University Munich and the Hebrew University of Jerusalem. He also writes as a guest blogger for the Times of Israel and serves as a volunteer at the Shiloh National Military Park.